Copyright © 2023 by Richard D. Wolff

All rights reserved.

No portion of this book may be reproduced in any form without written permission from the publisher or author, except as permitted by U.S. copyright law.

This publication is designed to provide accurate and authoritative information in regard to the subject matter covered. It is sold with the understanding that neither the author nor the publisher is engaged in rendering legal, investment, accounting or other professional services. While the publisher and author have used their best efforts in preparing this book, they make no representations or warranties with respect to the accuracy or completeness of the contents of this book and specifically disclaim any implied warranties of merchantability or fitness for a particular purpose. No warranty may be created or extended by sales representatives or written sales materials. The advice and strategies contained herein may not be suitable for your situation. You should consult with a professional when appropriate. Neither the publisher nor the author shall be liable for any loss of profit or any other commercial damages, including but not limited to special, incidental, consequential, personal, or other damages.

Book Cover by Amy Osika & Matthew Benetti

Illustrations by Amy Osika

First Edition 2024

Contents

Acknowledgements		2
Testimonials		4
Introduction		11
How to Read This Book		13
1.	Defining Capitalism: *What It Is*	15
	To understand capitalism, it will help if we first describe two non-capitalist systems	16
	The Employer/Employee Relationship	19
	Class	20
	Surplus	27
2.	Defining Capitalism: What It Is Not	37
	It Is Not Private Enterprise or Private Property	38
	Why Definitions Matter	44
3.	The Problems of Capitalism	47
	Undemocratic	49
	Unequal	53
	Unstable	60
	Instability & Debt in U.S. History	64
	Relations To Instability	68
	Inefficient	74
	Immoral	80
	Self-Destructive	87

4.	The Myths of Capitalism	93
	Capitalism Created Prosperity and Reduced Poverty	93
	Monopoly, Not Capitalism, Is the Problem	97
	Capitalism Is Uniquely Innovative	100
	Markets Are a Neutral, Efficient Way to Distribute Goods and Services	103
	Capitalism Enriches Those Who Deserve Riches	106
	Obscene Wealth is Justified by Huge Social Contributions	110
	Capitalists Deserve Profits Because They Take Risks	113
	Profit Best Motivates Production; Capitalism Exalts Profits	115
	Raising Wages Hurts Business and the Economy	117
	Capitalism Can Be Reformed	118
	Socialism Has Failed	122
5.	The Relationships of Capitalism	128
	Capitalism and the State	129
	Capitalism and Fascism	133
	Capitalism and Racism	139
	Capitalism and the Environment	143
6.	Capitalism and You	147
	You are Exploited	148
	Why So Many Hate Their Workplaces	148
	The "Do What You Love" Con	151
	The Ultimate Compensation for Labor Is Consumption	153
	Unemployment: Capitalism's Cruel Absurdity	154
	Capitalism and the Individual: Which Shapes Which?	155

	Individualism gone wrong	157
	Capitalism Trains you to Accept the Suffering of Others	160
	Living in the Contradictions of Capitalism	163
7.	What Comes After Capitalism	165
	Imagine a Better Way	166
	The Case for Worker Cooperation	168
	Worker Co-Ops Offer Democracy	170
	Co-Ops are Driven by More Than Profit	171
	Co-ops are a Force of Equality	172
	Translations Are Normal and Take Time We're Not Done Evolving	173
	Moving on From Capitalism	176

UNDERSTANDING CAPITALISM

Richard D. Wolff

Edited by Jayson T. Butler & Genisa Monroe

d@w DEMOCRACY AT WORK
FOR ECONOMIC JUSTICE

Acknowledgements

This book, like all books, is a collaboration (quite literally a working together) between the author(s) and a vast array of parents, teachers, students, colleagues and other "influencers." The dominant custom of crediting the author rather than the collaboration is a very particular way of reading and reaches correspondingly particular conclusions. The critical lens through which this book analyzes and understands capitalism depends on a lifelong engagement with the literature that assesses economic systems (capitalism especially, but also slavery, feudalism, socialism and so on). That lens is also shaped by a lifelong engagement with teaching economics in US universities and learning from my students. Most recently my colleagues in Democracy at Work, past and present, also contributed in various ways to producing this book: Ben August, Matt Binetti, Jayson T. Butler, Maria Carnemolla-Mania, Charles Fabian, Eric Halvarson, Shane Knight, Genisa Monroe, Amy Osika, Liz Phillips, Rob Robinson, and Giorgi Samushia. Discussions of the issues raised in this book with Dr. Harriet Fraad and with Tess Fraad-Wolff over decades distilled many of its central arguments as did similar discussions with my close friend and co-author, Stephen A. Resnick. Among my most important teachers were my father, Max Wolff, Fritz Pappenheim, Harry Magdoff, Paul M. Sweezy, Paul A Baran, Paul Tillich, Fred Jameson, Maurice Dobb, and Louis Althusser. I had valuable collaborative times with each of them.

3

Testimonials

Rick Wolff's analyses of economic systems are always right on point and very clear. In my opinion, he is the current best writer on Capitalism and related issues.

---- Dr. Richard A Rosen, Senior Fellow, Tellus Institute, retired

"When I first heard Prof. Wolff speak about workplace democracies, I realized I had never before encountered clearer, straightforward explanations of Socialism and Capitalism in my life. His work should be required reading for anyone navigating this dim, depressing hellscape of Capitalism and needs a light to guide them out of it."

---- Malaika Jabali, Author, *It's Not You, It's Capitalism: Why It's Time to Break Up, and How to Move On*

"Richard Wolff explains the big picture to those struggling to see our way through the complicated mess of the modern economic landscape. He simultaneously explains how huge the problems are while giving us hope that we can solve them. We're so lucky to have his wisdom at this time."

---- Marianne Williamson, Author, Speaker, Presidential Candidate

"The pathway from madness in our wrenching times! Wolff is our guardian guide through purgatory to clarity, courage, and action."

--- Dr. William Bronston, author, and medical care activist

"Dr. Richard Wolff is one of my favorite economists to interview. He is always well-informed, and his books challenge conventional ways of viewing economics."

--- Matthew Rozsa, staff writer at Salon Magazine and ABD at Lehigh University

"Richard Wolff's sharp insights and clear-eyed observations are especially invaluable now, as the world faces unparalleled crises and must plan for a radically different future. We should be grateful that his deep understanding of economics has not hindered his ability to read the writing on the wall."

---- Richard (RJ) Eskow, Journalist, Host of The Zero Hour with RJ Eskow

"If you ever wonder why so many economists contradict each other or why some things they say or write make no sense compared to the realities that you have experienced, then Professor Wolff's broadcasts, writings, and books are for you. We live in a world dominated by large corporations and extreme wealth and power inequalities, and only the type of analysis that Dr. Wolff offers can help us understand what is really happening. Powerful insights!"

---- Thomas E. Lambert, PhD, College of Business, University of Louisville

"Within these pages lies the remarkable journey of an industrious economist whose profound influence has reshaped our educational landscape. Delve into the story of relentless

dedication and transformative vision that has left an indelible mark on generations to come."

---- Nima R. Alkhorshid, Host of Podcast: Dialogue Works

Richard Wolff bears responsibility for restoring Socialism today to the center stage of popular political debate through a singular capacity to transmit Marxism to the public by clearly identifying the unfolding dialectical transformation and crisis of Capitalism.

--- Immanuel Ness, City University of New York

"Richard Wolff is one of the Left's most original thinkers and effective communicators. Over many years, he has demonstrated an unparalleled ability to use Marxian theory to critically analyze contemporary Capitalism and present his method and conclusions to a wide readership."

--- David F. Ruccio, Professor Emeritus at the University of Notre Dame

"Rick Wolff is the most influential Marxist economist in America! His rich intellectual range, from the decline of the American empire to the deeply racist character of predatory capitalist processes, is extraordinary! His courageous and analytical voice is a light in our grim times!"

--- Cornel West, Philosopher, Activist, and Professor, Union Theological Seminary

"Professor Wolff is my go-to source for all things economics. He dares reveal the cold hard truth that the capitalist zealots are blind to."

--- Lee Camp, journalist, comedian, activist

"College students are seeking conversations about alternative approaches to neoliberal economic and social life. They are eager to think and feel postcapitalist desires and experi-

ments. New imaginaries. Rick Wolff's weekly videos, occasional columns, and especially his books provide a thorough and open point of entry into a critique of our present that unleashes imaginaries of the future."

--- Lucas B Wilson, Professor of Economics and Critical race and political economy at the Ford Foundation, Mount Holyoke College

"Is anyone regularly updating the world on political economy with more forceful eloquence than Rick Wolff? Even where disagreements may arise, the power of Rick's pedagogy, clarity of his thought, and the overall impact he has together provide a model for us all."

--- Patrick Bond, Distinguished Professor and Director of the Centre for Social Change, University of Johannesburg)

"For decades Richard Wolff has remained one of the world's leading thinkers of Marxism, Socialism and Capitalism. More importantly, his body of work contains priceless theoretical resources for fundamentally transforming our understanding of these areas in the Southern context and in helping reimagine a postcapitalist future in the 21st century. Understanding Capitalism has found its best possible exponent."

--- Anjan Chakrabarti, Professor of Economics, University of Calcutta

"In a time of growing inequality and unchecked corporate power, Richard Wolff's lifelong work reminds us that another world is possible."

---Adam Hochschild, author

"Professor Wolff brings an incisive, critical perspective to the study of capitalism based on decades of research, as well as practical experience in organizing and activism; I highly recommend his work."

--- Asatar Bair, Professor of Economics, Riverside City College

"As capitalism's crises proliferate and accelerate, no one has written about their interconnectedness with greater clarity and insight than Richard Wolff. His new book, like its predecessors, moves beyond mere critique. It makes the case for economic planning, expanded public investment, and greater social ownership and democratic management of productive enterprises. Labor activists will find Understanding Capitalism to be an essential education tool."

--- Steve Early, Labor journalist, author, formerly with Communications Workers of America

"With this new book, Rick Wolff continues a longstanding project to show us that there are real, achievable alternatives to our contemporary economic and political malaise. It's not enough to know this isn't working. Wolff shows us why our economy is broken and how we can build a just, sustainable alternative that sustains us rather than divides us."

--- George DeMartino, Professor, Josef Korbel School of International Studies, University of Denver

"Across the nation and the world, people understand through lived experiences that this capitalist system isn't working for them. Professor Wolff gives language and expert analysis to what we all feel: Capitalism is a choice made by and for the few against and on the backs of the many. By taking purposefully obtuse concepts and boiling them down without any of the typical patronizing professorial pontifications, Wolff not only makes clear to us our shared enemy but gives us vital tools with which to fight it and, perhaps more importantly, to build something different - and better."

-- Eleanor Goldfield, Creative radical, journalist, and filmmaker

"Professor Wolff has a knack for writing in easy to digest language. As an activist and community organizer I enjoyed sharing the professor's work in communities across the globe. Understanding Capitalism will be another tool in this organizer's toolbox."

--- Rob Robinson Activist, Community Organizer and Professor of Urbanism, New School University, New York

"Rick Wolff has long been America's top Marxist public intellectual and the Left's invaluable treasure. His work appeals to the most serious students of the wreck we know as Capitalism, but it still inspires generation after generation of hopeful, energetic activists dedicated to changing out our class-biased, capitalist political economy for one more equitable. No one's theoretical or motivational work today comes similarly close in invigorating and galvanizing both young and old fighters for radical social change."

--- Jack Amariglio, Professor of Economics Emeritus, Merrimack College, Founding Editor of *Rethinking Marxism*

Richard Wolff is one of the most engaging and accessible economists out there. He makes what is all too often a dry and boring topic exciting and even fun.

--- Katie Halper, Host of The Katie Halper Show and co-host of Useful Idiots

Prof. Wolff is a prolific author and speaker whose particular forte is making complicated concepts simple, illuminated with practical illustrations that are easy to understand. He is particularly concerned with worker exploitation in the marketplace and with balancing capitalist economic freedom with socialist fair and equal treatment.

---Ellen Brown, founder and chairman of the Public Banking Institute, a nonpartisan think tank devoted to the creation of publicly run banks

Introduction

For as long as we have had capitalism, people have disagreed about what it is. Some have loved capitalism, some have hated it, and many have been curious about how it works and why. Not surprisingly, different definitions shape different feelings about capitalism, and vice versa. Allow me to explain why I chose to write a book that defines capitalism today.

Nowadays, many people have realized that the capitalist system is riddled with problems, but they lack a grasp of basic concepts in economics. Those concepts are needed to understand why capitalism had these problems and to evaluate the different "solutions" offered. Basic economics literacy is notoriously low in most parts of the world. School courses, politicians' statements, and mainstream media have often confused or mystified people about how capitalism works. They have often also misled people by failing to explain the radically different ways different people define and understand capitalism.

Here, our goal is to understand capitalism. So we begin with a basic definition that we can use to understand it. However, this definition also enables us to explain *how* and *why* others see capitalism differently. This book is intended for all readers: those who like capitalism, those who don't, and those still undecided.

Over its roughly five centuries, capitalism spread to become the truly global system it is today. It has been widely celebrated and widely criticized. The same happened to slavery, feudalism, and all the other economic systems humans have tried. Sooner or later, intelligent people inside all systems grasped that to understand any system requires carefully considering the perspective of both those who celebrate it and those who do not. Watching, listening to, or reading only either one yields a one-sided perspective closer to propaganda than to genuine understanding. This book offers a critical point of view that is all too often overlooked, denied, or silenced. It offers that to those honest enough to dare to really consider both sides, rather than engage with yet another book that cheerleads for capitalism instead of understanding it.

I cannot claim to be neutral in today's challenging situation. Very, very few people truly are. While most economists are pro-capitalist—as are most politicians, media representatives, and academics in the US and beyond—I am among the critics of capitalism. I became a critic because I saw the everyday realities of this system grinding most people down for the benefit of the few.

I'm convinced humans can do better than the existing system. The world is going through so many crises—war, climate change, wealth inequality, mass migration, and civil unrest—and meeting with few successes. I believe that understanding capitalism—the basic economic system of our times—offers us the key to addressing these crises successfully.

How to Read This Book

The capitalism in which we all live and struggle is in trouble. You, the reader, are rightly interested in understanding why and how the system is connected to all this trouble. I wrote this book to help you do exactly that.

But no book's writing occurs in a vacuum. Our world is full of different and often clashing views about the capitalist system. Whether you admire capitalism or criticize it (or some of both), the terms and definitions you use change depending on your opinion.

That means that writers who seek to be clear must define in their own terms how they understand key concepts and ideas. I do that here in the first two chapters. I then proceed to use those defined terms to analyze capitalism as a system (with special reference to the sources of its present difficulties or troubles).

The opening chapters, on what capitalism *is* and *is not*, may be a bit challenging. The beginnings of analysis often are. Definitions of key concepts and basic ideas seem far less interesting than what these concepts tell us about the world that we live in—which is what we do with the topics covered in the rest of the book.

The exciting and urgent issues about capitalism occupy its main, major portions. You can see that in the detailed table of contents. This book is critical in the sense that I do not shy away from examining capitalism's flaws and weaknesses, because they are important sources of its problems. Criticism also carries the obligation to discuss solutions: both reforms of the system and transition to another system. The approach here does both.

Chapter One

Defining Capitalism: What It Is

Across capitalism's history, as it spread from England in the seventeenth century to become global today, its interactions with different nations, cultures, and economic conditions led to different understandings of capitalism. The world is now awash in different meanings of the basic terms, concepts, and words we use to describe our economic systems. The notions of right and wrong are not appropriate here; different people can define terms they find useful in different ways.

Here we define "capitalism" as the name of one particular way that human communities have organized the production of the goods and services on which they depend. Ranging in size from families to nations or the entire world, all communities produce goods and services. History shows that human communities have organized their production systems in different ways in different times and places.

Each of these particular production systems arises, evolves, and passes away. Sometimes they spread to other places. Sometimes multiple production systems exist in one place at a time.

Today, capitalism is the dominant production system across most of the world. It emerged from and spread during the decline of Europe's previous production system, called *feudalism*. Centuries earlier, that feudal production system had emerged from the decline and collapse of yet another production system, *slavery*.

Capitalism, we presume, will follow the same path as other systems. Rising out of the decline of previous production systems such as slavery and feudalism, capitalism grew and evolved. Eventually, capitalism too will pass away, and another production system will take its place.

To understand capitalism, it will help if we first describe two non-capitalist systems.

Let's start with slavery. That production system organizes its participants into two connected groups: masters and slaves. Their basic relationship is summarized by the fact that masters own slaves as property and thus wield power over them. The slaves do most of the work but are excluded from deciding what to produce, how and where the work is done, and what to do with the end products. The other group, masters, makes all those decisions. The slaves are not free; they don't even own themselves. Masters control everything—even the slave's participation in the system.

The masters take and distribute all of the slave system's produced goods and services, such as the crops slaves plant and pick. One portion of the slaves' output is typically sold by the master who owns it. The master then uses the resulting revenue from selling the slaves' output to purchase replacements for the inputs used up in production, such as seeds and tools. A second portion of the slaves' output, such as food, goes directly from the master to sustain the slaves and their families. Masters sell the remaining portion and keep the resulting revenue as their own income.

In slavery, masters could limit the portion of the slaves' output that they returned to the slaves' for their consumption. Often, masters *did* limit or reduce this portion returned to slaves because that left a bigger portion for the masters. Because of that built-in incentive, masters often abused the slaves they owned and brutally repressed slaves' opposition or efforts to escape. Eventually, slave resistance undermined the system. Relatively few instances of the slave production system remain in today's world.

Another non-capitalist production system, European feudalism, organizes its participants differently, into lords and serfs. The serfs do most of the work, while the lords make all the key decisions. However, unlike slavery, the serf is not considered to be property of the lords. Instead, the feudal system connects lords and serfs within a religious social order that establishes and enforces a particular relationship between lord and serf. The lord presides over the land, distributes portions of the land to serfs, and protects the serfs so that they can work the land. In return, the serfs must obey the lord and also deliver a portion of the output they produce (such as crops) to the lord. The rest of the serfs' output they can keep for themselves and their families.

Much like slavery, feudal lords take the outputs delivered to them by their serfs and use them as they choose. If markets exist, lords may sell those delivered outputs for money/revenue. One part of such revenue goes to the lord's consumption (building castles, organizing feasts, etc.). Another part might be used to purchase and replace inputs used in the production activities of the serfs (tools, equipment, etc.). Lords would distribute another part of their revenue to the church and the king to secure their efforts to support the whole feudal system.

Like slavery, the feudal production system was eventually undone by serfs refusing to accept it. They resisted and tried to escape. While feudalism rejected the concept and institution of slavery, feudalism's legally "free" serfs suffered and resented their system's deep inequalities. Eventually, it too broke down.

These are straightforward explanations of these systems. But, the reality is that human communities have organized their production systems in multiple ways, even during the same period in history. While each production system can exist alone in a community, coexistence among several is more usual.

For example, slave and feudal systems can and do coexist with capitalism. The US Constitution's Thirteenth Amendment explicitly allows for slavery to exist inside US prisons. Likewise, some traditional US households and family farms are organized around the husband/father as lord (of his castle), with the wife and older children as serfs. Participants may not recognize the slave or feudal organization of their families and households, and they may not use those words to define their situation, but that does not prevent slavery or feudalism from being their reality.

These are simply possible examples; there is no necessity for slavery or feudalism to coexist within an economy where capitalism is the prevalent economic system.

So, what exactly is the unique production relationship defining capitalism? The answer offered here represents what I have found to be the most effective definition, in terms of the understanding of capitalism it makes possible.

The Employer/Employee Relationship

In its best-known form, the capitalist production relationship connects employers to employees by means of an exchange contract. Employees sell their capacity to work (their *labor power*) to employers for a wage. Employers set employees to work with means of production (tools, equipment, raw materials, etc.) that employers usually own. Employers organize the work to produce specific outputs.

Capitalism's distinctive production relationship excludes the human ownership of slavery and the interpersonal obligations of feudalism. Instead of masters and slaves or lords and serfs, we have employers and employees.

The particular capitalist relationship differs from the slave and feudal relationships in this way: in slavery and feudalism, the buying and selling of labor power do not exist; in them, labor power is not a commodity. Many forms of slavery and feudalism have markets in productive resources, products, and even enslaved persons (within chattel slavery). But, none of those forms have a market where one group sells their labor power to another. The exchange of labor power is one unique activity that comprises a different productive relationship, namely that of capitalism.

Capitalism's employer–employee exchange comes with a condition: the employer owns the output of the labor process automatically, as fast as the employees produce it.

In modern capitalism, the marketplace is most often the main mechanism of distribution of produced output. Most resources and products are owned by employers who buy and sell resources/products as commodities, alongside buying and selling labor power as another commodity.

The employees use their wage payments to buy the consumer goods needed to reproduce their own labor power (food, clothing, housing, education, health care). What employees consume is what employees produce. Employers occupy a middle position between employees while wielding decisive power (in capitalism) over employees.

The contractual relationship binding employers and employees differentiates capitalism from alternative production systems. Yet the capitalist system also shares some important qualities with slavery and feudalism. For example, like them, in capitalism a very small minority of the people involved in each workplace—the employers (aka the owner, the board of directors, the major shareholders)—decide what most workplaces produce, what technology they use, and what is done with the workplaces' profits. Employees, the vast majority in most workplaces, are excluded from making those decisions. Yet employees must live with those decisions' consequences (rather like slaves and serfs must live with the decisions made exclusively by masters and lords, respectively). Their very unequal divisions of authority within workplaces have been fundamental problems for slavery, feudalism, and capitalism.

Class

Here, I introduce and define the term "class" because this book uses class in a particular way.

Many folks think of class in terms of power and wealth. Defining class in terms of power, many people say that societies are divided among groups with different amounts of power over others. Some people can order other people to do or behave in certain ways. Such people are said to have authority: to be "order-givers" rather than "order-takers." In contrast, other people are said to be without authority: to be order-takers rather than order-givers. The word "class" has often been used to describe such groups: the powerful ruling class (those who give orders) versus the powerless or ruled class (those who take orders). In between them, we find middle classes: groups that have some power but not as much as those in the ruling class which have a lot.

Class has also been used in a parallel way to describe the division of wealth in a society or nation or community. The rich comprise the upper class, while the poor comprise the lower class. Of course, there can be middle classes whose wealth or income is somewhere between rich and poor.

For many centuries, people have used these power or wealth concepts of class to understand why communities work and change in particular ways. Critics of social problems have often pointed to class differences as being their major causes and proposed class changes as solutions. Supporters of democracy have argued that its survival depends on most people in any community being in the middle classes, relatively equal in wealth and power.

The fact is that for a long time, many attempts have been made to overcome class differences as one key way to build a better society for all. Successes have so far been only partial and temporary. Extreme class differences—in both power and wealth—continue to be widespread from the US to China, from the global North to the global South. Many have tried to understand this problem. Why has it been so very difficult to avoid or end extreme class differences in wealth and power?

One approach to answering this key question derives from the work of the famed philosopher, economist, and social critic Karl Marx.

He believed that other social thinkers who had sincerely wanted to overcome extreme class differences failed to do so because they had missed or misunderstood a key cause of those differences.

So important did Marx consider his discovery that he built a whole analysis of capitalism around it. In effect, Marx invented a new concept of class—a new definition—that he then used to analyze capitalism. He knew the previous concepts of class—those defined in terms of wealth and power distributions—but he added, elaborated, and applied his new concept to them.

Marx's approach divides the people engaged in the capitalist production system into two groups. One group is employers; the other is employees. This is a different way of "classifying" people. Classes are not about how much wealth they do or do not own or how much power they do or do not wield. Class, for Marx, is about a person's position in a production system.

Marx's unique class-analytical approach to understanding capitalism spread quickly in his lifetime, and even faster after his death in 1883. In its many interpretations, Marxism became a major global tradition of social thought. This book uses Marx's idea of class because of the unique and powerful insights it offers into capitalism.

The employer class is extremely small. In the US, their numbers are variously estimated (depending on the methods used) at between 1 and 3 percent of the adult workforce. Estimates of the total number of US businesses hover around thirty-three million (but most of those are individual self-employed enterprises). In contrast, the US labor force (a rough measure of all "employees") is approximately 165 million people (about half the US population). In class terms, the key reality here is that there is a small class of employers compared to the much larger class of employees.

Our adult population is mostly employees. Right there is a fundamental problem. Employers decide what to produce, where to produce it, how to produce it, and what to do with output (that belongs to them). Because employees are not slaves or serfs, they are free to quit an employer and to offer to another their capacity to work. Employers are free to accept or reject any such offers, to hire and to fire. But, employees do not share with employers the rights to control the production process, nor what to do with the products of the employees' labor. Employers retain those rights exclusively for themselves.

In the capitalist production system, then, one class wields huge powers denied to the other class. Each of the two classes' powers emerges or derives from their different positions within the organization of production. If a society were, in general, to be committed to democracy—to a "one person, one vote," equal distribution of political power—capitalism's very different organization of production (not at all "one person, one vote") would present an immediate, obvious problem (a point discussed in detail later in this book, in "The Problems of Capitalism: Undemocratic").

Marx's class analysis can be applied to non-capitalist economic systems. In slavery and feudalism, the top classes (masters and lords) gathered into their hands hugely disproportional shares of wealth and power. Critics of those systems railed against their extreme inequalities of wealth and power. Marx's concept of class again focused on their production systems to explain how those systems distributed wealth and power.

When slaves and serfs refused to continue within slave and feudal productive systems, they demanded "freedom" from those systems, and many embraced capitalism as the way forward to a "free society." Employees were neither slaves nor serfs. Employees were free and only voluntarily entered into the capitalist production system. This could be seen as an improvement from the previous systems. Yet capitalism's employees were also those who worked, produced, and generated wealth that employers took and distributed to keep the capitalist production system going.

Marx's new class analysis, focused on the employer/employee relationship, enabled him to pinpoint what had to be changed—in all production systems, including capitalism—to end the wealth and power inequalities those systems all shared. *Any* production system that positioned a small minority in charge of a large majority had to be changed.

Capitalism's champions had promised their system would end the inequalities of wealth and power associated with slavery and feudalism. Capitalism they insisted, would bring about liberty, equality, and democracy. Marx argued that capitalism failed to deliver on its promises because, in place of the master/slave and lord/serf dichotomies, it installed the employer/employee system. To achieve the promises of capitalism requires going beyond employer/employee to a new production system that does *not* divide the people engaged in production into the powerful versus the powerless, the rich and the poor. The capitalist organization of the workplace is the obstacle to realizing the noble goals of capitalism's original champions.

In capitalist, feudal, and slave production systems, Marx noted, the workers (employees, serfs, slaves) produce "surpluses" for persons other than themselves. That is, they produce a quantity of output greater than that necessary to provide for those employees' standards of consumption and to replace used-up means of production. The difference between total outputs produced by slaves, serfs, and employees and what each of those classes received for their own consumption plus used-up inputs was what Marx called "surpluses." Because all such workers produced surpluses for others (for masters, lords, and employers, but not for themselves), Marx referred to them as "exploited."

Progressive critics of capitalism have always opposed exploitation as perhaps capitalism's fundamental injustice. Yet the very idea or concept of exploitation immediately brings to mind the question: What would a nonexploitative production system be? The answer this book provides is the worker cooperative: a workplace where the relationship among participants is a democratic community. Each participant in the activities of the workplace has one vote in making its basic decisions: what, how, and where to produce and how to utilize the output of the workplace. The surplus produced by such a workers' cooperative would *not* be immediately taken by others. It would instead belong to and be distributed by the workers who produced it. (See the discussion of this key point in the last chapter of this book, entitled "What Comes After Capitalism?")

Exploitative economic systems like slavery and feudalism prevented the dreams of liberty, equality, and democracy from becoming realities. Capitalism promised to make these dreams a reality, but it failed. And Marx's work exposed why: capitalism, too, had installed an exploitative economic system.

The good news is that we now know what needs to be done. We need to transition our economic system from its capitalist (i.e., employer/employee) organization of workplaces to democratically organized worker cooperatives. We must end capitalist exploitation, much as our ancestors ended slavery and feudalism.

Capital

Why, you may rightly wonder, is capitalism not called "the employer/employee system" or some other phrase that describes its specific qualities as a production system? The answer is historical.

The concepts of *capital* and *capitalist* long predated the existence and spread of the employer/employee production system. Put simply, those concepts referred to one particular use of money: using money to make more money.

Money can be used to purchase something to make practical use of it (as in buying something to consume it). Money could also be given as a gift. This money would *not* be called capital. What is capital is money when it is used to generate *more* money. Capital, in other words, is self-expanding money.

Think of a value of money—say $100—that is used in a way that ends up with its owner having more than $100. The simplest example is money loaned at interest. The borrower is then required to return the value of the loan *plus 5 percent interest* (a fee charged to the borrower). A one-year $100 loan will yield $105 a year later (return of principal, $100, plus a $5 interest payment). Lending money at interest turns that money into capital.

Another simple example is using money as storekeepers or merchants do. They buy in order to resell *at a higher price.* Your corner store buys potato chips at a (wholesale) price that's lower than what it charges you (the retail price). In this way, the store owner expands the value of money: money used as capital.

Please note that neither loan capital nor merchant capital directly involves production. The loan with interest involves the change of ownership of money between lender and borrower, not the production of anything. A merchant's business of buying low and selling high involves no production either. As you can see, production is a separate activity from these forms of capital, and it happens before any merchant buys and resells what was earlier produced.

For most of human history, production was not primarily done to make money. In all previous eras, production was motivated by all sorts of goals, but it was not primarily driven by capital, the attempt to use money to make more money.

A whole new era of human history began when capital grew beyond lending and merchanting and became directly engaged in production. The employer/employee organization of production not only replaced earlier slave and feudal organizations of production but also brought capital into the center of the production system. It was properly called a capitalist production system because "making money" was its logic, its "law of motion," and its "bottom line."

How does money's self-expansion occur within the employer/employee relationship?

Surplus

When an employer puts a hired laborer to work with equipment and raw materials to make a product, the employer expends a total sum of money to buy and gather all those components into a workplace or enterprise. Because an employer uses money to produce with the goal of expanding value, that money is "capital", and such an employer is a capitalist. The goal is to end the production process with something worth more in value than the total sum of value the employer put into production in the first place.

What is critical to understand here is that the value grows during capitalist production because of the employer/employee relationship.

The value of the product includes the values of all the component inputs used up in the process of production (the used-up equipment, facilities, and raw materials). The employee's labor adds to those inputs' value to yield the total value of production's output. The product of production is worth more than the value of the used-up inputs that are contained in it. The increased value comes from what the labor adds.

Now, here comes the key point.

The employer (or someone designated by the employer) manages the production process to make money. But exactly how does the employer end up with more value in the product than the employer expended on the inputs plus the cost of getting the laborer to work? The answer is this: the employer must be able to pay a wage or salary to the employee that has *less value* than that added by the worker's labor during production. The output of capitalist production *includes* the value added by the worker, but it only *costs* the employer the value of the wage that the worker requires to perform the work. The value added by the worker's labor minus the value paid to the worker as a wage is the "surplus." The employer spends value on production that equals the value of the used-up inputs plus the value of the wage paid to the worker. The employer realizes the value of the output (when it is sold) that contains (1) the value of the used-up inputs, plus (2) the value paid to the worker for working, and (3) the surplus (or excess of worker's value added over the wage paid).

The difference between the value added by laborers and wages paid to them is the key to capitalism. It is that "more" that enables money or value to self-expand by means of capitalist production. The "more" (originally *mehr* in Marx's German-language writings) was translated into English as "surplus."

UNDERSTANDING CAPITALISM

Thus "surplus value" is the goal and driver of the employer/employee production system; it is quite literally what makes it capitalist. Employers get the surplus produced by their employees. As it is produced, it becomes the employers' property. That happens automatically. Many capitalists and many employees never quite grasp or understand the system that connects them.

If the employer decides to keep the enterprise going (exclusively the employer's decision), that employer must use the revenue from selling its outputs (which belong exclusively to that employer) in particular ways. One portion of the revenue buys physical inputs to replenish those used up in production. A second portion is paid in wages to the employees who produced those products. A third and final portion—the surplus value—is used by the employer to secure certain conditions needed for the enterprise to keep going.

These conditions include, for example, hiring lawyers to manage any legal issues that might impede the enterprise's reproduction over time or paying taxes to the state so it can maintain services on which the employer relies (roads, police, public education, etc.).

Still another condition would be hiring employees who do *not* produce surplus but instead perform functions that enable surpluses to be produced by other employees. For example, let's consider a ladder factory that hires a clerk to manage the paperwork to keep track of payroll, billing, or legal obligations. The clerk produces neither ladders nor the surplus that ladder-producing workers do. Yet the clerk is as important to a successful capitalist enterprise as the direct ladder-producer (the one who uses tools and equipment to transform wood into ladders). Employees like this clerk are *enablers*: they enable other workers to produce the surplus that drives the capitalist enterprise. The enabler class in capitalism includes such workers as clerks, sales personnel, security, supervisors, and so on. So now we see that capitalism entails a complex class structure. Employees include both surplus-producing workers and non-surplus-producing enablers.

In the long history of economics, key contributors such as Adam Smith and Karl Marx referred to these groups as "productive" and "unproductive" workers. While they defined these terms differently, they all aimed analytically to break down the important category of wage-earning employees. Even everyday language has tried to grasp such differences among workers with terms like "white collar" and "blue collar." In this book, "productive" workers are those who directly produce the surpluses that employers aim to maximize. Unproductive workers are those who help create the conditions that enable productive workers to produce surpluses.

The difference between "productive" and "unproductive" does *not* refer to the importance of these two groups of workers. Both groups are indispensable to the survival and persistence of the capitalist enterprise, albeit in different ways. We differentiate the two groups in terms of their relationships to the surplus because it helps us understand capitalism according to this book's definition.

The lower the wages employers can pay to any worker, the greater the share of workers' value added that employers take as surplus. Capitalism—the employer/employee organization of production—thus sets employers against employees. Lower wages are typically pursued by employers and resisted by employees. In contrast, employees perpetually seek to increase wages to improve their families' standards of living. Capitalism has always been a system torn by internal conflicts and struggles between employers and employees.

These economic conflicts and struggles influence and are shaped by the politics and culture of every society where the capitalist economic system prevails. Do schools teach children about how capitalism works? Is labor unionization fostered or demonized in the culture?

Do political struggles mobilize public opinion to support one class against another, or do they deflect popular opinion away from class issues so as to support the class status quo? The ways such questions are answered show how those and other aspects of society shape how much surplus each enterprise's employers can appropriate, and how successfully those employers can use those surpluses to hire and direct the enablers to do their part.

Profit

We know that the profit drive is the heart of capitalism. That's why businesses say things like "Profit is our bottom line," "We're in business to make profit," or a hundred other ways of saying it. But what exactly is profit? Two particular distributions of surplus by employers became so important that a special term was invented for them: "profit."

The first version of "profit" refers to when surplus is used to grow or expand the enterprise: (1) to buy more or different physical inputs instead of simply replenishing those used up, and (2) to hire more employees to work with those inputs and produce more output.

The other particular distribution of surplus labeled "profit" is made to the owners of the enterprise: a kind of "return" on the capital such owners had made available to ("invested in") the enterprise.

Profit became a kind of shorthand index for how well a capitalist enterprise was doing because it measured how much surplus value was left over after the employer had secured all the other necessary conditions to continue producing. Profit was that part of the surplus that employers could distribute to owners of the enterprise for two specific purposes: (i) for owner(s)' consumptions and (ii) to increase owners' wealth (by growing the enterprise). Profit reflected and thus measured how successfully an employer had operated a capitalist enterprise.

We would better analyze an enterprise by looking at *all* distributions of surplus. Profit is after all just two among that became the key number capitalists use to gauge each enterprise's financial health. Indeed, there are other distributions of surplus that are also important for its future.

It is easy to slip into the habit of treating "surplus" and "profit" as interchangeable, as synonyms. In some cases, that incurs no confusion; in others, it does. In one important way, surplus and profit can be considered together despite their differences. All surplus distributions—including profits—are important ways to secure an enterprise's continuation or reproduction. Inadequate distribution of portions of the surplus risks not reproducing capitalism's conditions, thereby threatening the enterprise's survival.

A major problem for capitalists is the nature of their relationship with one another. That relationship includes competition. What each capitalist does to be profitable, reproduce, and even grow can, and usually does, threaten the existence of other capitalists. Thus, capitalists seek profits both to defend against their competitors and to obtain advantages over them.

For example, consider a group of capitalist enterprises that produce and sell chairs to the same community of buyers. The interactions between the multiple businesses selling into their shared market creates a pressure expressed by the term "competition." In order to survive, each business must sell outputs for revenues which it then uses to replenish used-up inputs, pay wages, and distribute its surplus value to secure the conditions needed to reproduce the enterprise. Each capitalist chair-producer faces the risk that chair buyers will patronize another "competing" business. Each capitalist seeks ways to take business away from its competitors. It can, and often does, become a life-and-death struggle.

Competition might drive one capitalist to improve the quality of its chairs and/or reduce their price. To sustain its profitsm such a capitalist would try to find cheaper productive inputs. Alternatively, that same capitalist might send less of its surplus to secure conditions of that enterprise's existence, such as security guards, secretaries, etc. Every other chair capitalist, threatened by the first's improved quality or lowered price, would pursue the same or comparable steps. "Competition" is what we call this tense coexistence. It's a constant pressure on and danger to capitalists. As we shall see, it also underlies capitalists' endless quest for growth. A bigger enterprise is often better able to compete than a smaller one.

That is how capitalism works. Profits are usually devoted partly or wholly to growing the enterprise. Capitalist enterprises are profit driven because profit is often what fuels growth. Expansion is itself a condition of enterprise's competitive survival. More employees producing outputs means more surplus to secure conditions of the enterprise's existence and reproduction.

Companies are terrified if their profits go down. Will people then stop investing in the company? Will vendors with whom they do business stop extending credit? Will customers begin to look elsewhere (maybe to competitors)? Might banks hesitate to lend to the company?

Profit has thus become a key marker, measure, and criterion of the health of every capitalist enterprise. Rising profits as a share of total capital invested (a rising *profit rate*) is good news for vendors, lenders, and investors that the capitalist enterprise deals with. Profits are what the media consider when commenting on an enterprise's condition and prospects. Falling profits send the same audience the opposite news. Corporate executives' jobs tend to be more secure and better paid when profits are rising. However, recent decades have shown that top US executives obtain improved salaries and bonuses even when their enterprises' profits fall.

Capitalism's "high priests"—the professional economists—spin the tales (they prefer to call them theories) that justify the system. They try to persuade us that capitalists' "profit maximization" achieves the greatest efficiency, economic growth, and the greatest good for the greatest number of people. They want us to believe that the self-serving (profit-driven) behavior of the employer class is, magically, the best for employees too.

It is always difficult to keep track of the multiple causes of profit. Thus, many choose to focus instead on one or two "key" causes or aspects. Across capitalism's history, the *hope* that profits show an enterprise's overall economic health became the *presumption* that they do. Average profits across industries and entire economies likewise became indices of economic well-being.

One immediate problem with such a standard or measure is that it opens the possibility that profits may be high and rising because wages, taxes, and living conditions are falling. Is such a capitalist system healthy or not? If profit earners (a tiny minority) own and run the media, politicians, and academics, that minority's well-being may result in the "news" that the economy is prospering. If most people live off wages and salaries and the decline of the latter imposes suffering on them, they might find the same economy to be the opposite of prosperous. Nothing about profit is neutral or the same for all in society; it is a highly contested concept, as are all basic economic concepts if one looks at them closely.

Capitalists don't focus on profit because they are greedy. Rather, greed is another name for the profit drive that competition requires and thus cultivates in capitalists. The capitalist system *imposes* profit-driven behavior upon individual capitalists. If and when individual employers adapt to capitalism's profit drive, we may call them "greedy," but the system shapes and imposes on the individual far more than the reverse. The capitalist system's profit drive is the cause; greediness is the effect. Of course, the effect can and does react back upon its cause. Greedy individual employers may become capitalist employers and perhaps excel in profit-making.

For every example where profit-driven behavior leads to a good outcome, there is another that exposes profit-driven behavior leading to awful outcomes. The profit drive may have resulted in dynamic technological improvements, but this also helped cause colonialism, imperialism, and some of the most destructive wars in human history. It now even threatens our ecological survival. The profit motive yields, at best, mixed results. To imagine that profit magically guides economies to optimal goodness, growth, and prosperity, is above all capitalists' wishful thinking.

Profit maximization is how capitalists accumulate wealth. That may be good for them, but it's not at all good for the rest of us. Keeping profits away from employees guarantees they will always need employment from capitalists, locking employees in a cycle of exploitation and dependence on wages. Capitalists and workers have never been equal beneficiaries of the system.

So that's capitalism: employers use employees to produce surplus and profit, and employers distribute the surplus for their own benefit and, under the pressure of competition, for the growth (or at least reproduction) of their enterprises.

Knowing now what capitalism is, we should ask ourselves an important question: What are we doing allowing our very lives and societal well-being to depend on the decisions of a tiny minority who forever prioritize that one small portion of enterprise revenue called profit?

Before we can invest ourselves in this question, I'm guessing there may be some questions or counterarguments forming in your mind.

We can address those by unraveling some other definitions of capitalism that you may have heard of.

Chapter Two

Defining Capitalism: What It Is Not

The task of defining anything includes separating what it is from what it is not. That means we must define boundaries between an object and its surroundings. We define a "dog" as an "animal," but we must also show how it differs from other animals, like a "cat." The boundaries comprising a definition are crucial to understanding "dog" because "animal" is not enough. The same applies to defining capitalism. To be clear about what this economic system is, we have to separate it from others.

This chapter's discussion of what capitalism *is not* will add those clarifying boundaries to its definition. This is especially important because these boundaries will also help us separate the very different ways capitalism has been understood.

It Is Not Private Enterprise or Private Property

Most advocates of capitalism heavily emphasize what is "private"—what is "mine," "yours," or "someone else's." To them, capitalism is a system of "free" or "private" enterprises and private ownership: a system where private individuals start, own, and operate enterprises mostly free of government interference and where those individuals decide how to run enterprises or what to do with them.

First of all, private or free enterprises existed in most slave or feudal economic systems. They are not unique to and thus do not define capitalism. Individuals often could and did buy slaves, setting them to work in private enterprises that operated in classic master/slave fashion. The same happened often in feudalism as private individuals entered into lord–serf relationships within feudal enterprises. Whatever distinguishes capitalist from other enterprises, their "private" or "free" nature is not it.

It is, of course, possible for a state to set up and operate a business enterprise. State officials can buy inputs and hire workers, produce and sell outputs. In virtually all societies that have ever called themselves capitalist, states have done that. In the US, examples are many: the US Postal Service, Amtrak, the Tennessee Valley Authority, thousands of local utilities owned by municipalities, states operating colleges and universities, and so on. Most citizens and commentators do not deny the US is capitalist because of those state-owned-and-operated businesses. To be fair, a few people do those for whom any state-owned-and-run enterprise is a negation of capitalism.

Slavery and feudalism, like capitalism, exhibited coexistences of private and state enterprises. Virtually no student of slavery ever concluded that slavery ceased to exist when states joined individuals in buying slaves and setting them to work. Likewise, students of feudalism around the world noted that states as well as private lords operated feudal production systems. Such students did *not* conclude that feudalism had been abolished when states joined private enterprises.

A relatively small number of people—in the US today, they take the name "libertarians"—believe that the private-versus-state difference defines capitalism. Their evident hatred for state apparatuses is clearly reflected in their way of defining capitalism.

Most nations labeled as "capitalist" actually include both private and state enterprises; so too do most nations labeled as "socialist." The proportions of private versus state enterprises vary from nation to nation, from time to time within nations, and likewise within systems. Thus, the private-versus-state difference is not a clear way to separate economic systems; it is weak as a definition.

Capitalism does not uniquely incentivize private enterprise either. Capitalism has its own ways of preventing private enterprises from forming. For example, with typical patent and trademark systems, capitalists who develop something new can forbid other capitalists from making the same thing for many years. Also, capitalist competition drives employers to control the market and stop other enterprises from entering the industry. These are ways that capitalism often blocks or thwarts private enterprises. Other noncapitalist systems likewise incentivize and disincentivize the formation of enterprises, both private and state.

Private property is not unique to capitalism either. Once again, private property coexists with state or collective property within slave, feudal, and other production systems, just like capitalist systems. As with enterprises, the relative quantities of private versus nonprivate property in each production system may vary over time and across places. Land, animals, machines, money, and much else have long histories as both private and state property in many different systems.

Accusing anti-capitalists of generally opposing or abolishing private property is historically inaccurate. However, there are political and ideological goals in defining anti-capitalism in such terms. The accusation that socialism, for example, is anti-private property scares some people, who believe that socialism somehow threatens their private belongings. Not only is that mostly untrue but there are examples in capitalist systems when private property is rejected. The US legal principle of eminent domain grants the government the right to take private property from its owners without their consent and convert it into state property so long as "fair compensation" is paid for it. US capitalism has thus recognized the legitimacy of state property and the curtailment of private property.

Equating capitalism with private property is a mistake.

It Is Not Markets

Markets, too, are not unique to capitalism, nor do they define it. Yet many persist in referring to capitalism as "the market system" or the "free market."

Markets are a way of distributing goods and services that preceded capitalism by many centuries. Markets enable producers to transfer their products to consumers by means of exchange. If sellers and buyers can reach an agreement on the terms of their exchange, products change hands.

Plato and Aristotle wrote about markets and their social effects in the fourth century BC. (and they both criticized markets). Markets often began as sporadic events occurring at the edges of communities and then sometimes matured into regular events integrated into the lives of communities and entire regions. Markets accommodated both long- and short-distance trade and traders. In slave societies, slaves were often bought and sold in markets alongside products of slave labor. In feudalism, products of serf labor were also bought and sold in marketplaces.

Perhaps to differentiate capitalism from these earlier markets, some folks claim capitalism is "the free market system," with "free" meaning a market system with minimal or no outside (i.e., governmental) intervention or regulation. In such "free" markets, buyers and sellers bargain unregulated by any political authority.

The problem is, such free markets existed rarely and only briefly. Most markets are full of regulations imposed upon market exchanges, usually by governments.

Consider a labor market where businesses pay very little and desperate people must accept low wages. Very poor people have eventually demanded help in the form of a market regulation mandating a legally enforced minimum wage. For example, the nineteenth- and twentieth-century labor market for immigrants working on farms in the US gave employers the power to impose on employed farmworkers both awful conditions and low wages. The supply of desperate immigrants was large, and US farm employers were ruthless in their drive for profits. Immigrant workers' efforts to regulate that market were defeated by employers' counter-efforts for a long time, but eventually, through great struggle, unions like the United Farm Workers of America arose, and won government-imposed protective regulations. Their successful advocacy for better working conditions and a higher minimum wage reflects unions' understanding of markets as a human invention they try to shape to their needs.

Capitalism once displayed armies of child laborers who were paid poorly and treated badly. Eventually, workers fought against this practice, and regulations banned child labor, thereby intervening in capitalism's labor markets. Sexual abuse of employees, ecological damages, deceptive products, and countless other factors demanded and eventually got government regulation of capitalist markets. Unregulated "free" markets are much more a utopian ideal than an existing reality across the history of markets.

Long ago, Aristotle and Plato argued that markets undermine social cohesion—what we might now call "community." They agreed in their critiques of markets, but they disagreed over what to do about markets' socially undesirable effects. For example, markets favor the rich. The rich can more easily afford the means to become richer. Markets thus can, and often do, worsen the inequality of wealth among members of the community. That, in turn, provokes envy and jealousy among them. It also provokes the rich to use their wealth to protect that wealth by influencing politicians and mass media in ways the poor cannot match. Debaters since Plato and Aristotle have often agreed with their criticisms of markets and likewise disagreed over whether to simply ban market exchange or else to regulate it. (The chapter "Myths of Capitalism," later in this book, further details these harmful effects of markets.)

While markets in general are not unique to capitalism, the market for one particular product was so unique to capitalism that it has become definitional. That particular commodity is labor power. In capitalism, the worker sells labor power: the capacity to contribute brains and muscles to production. The worker owns and sells labor power to the capitalist employer. The capitalist buys and then "consumes" that labor power by combining the worker with tools, equipment, and raw materials to produce a product. The capitalist owns and sells that product. The labor power market is the only market that does not typically occur in other systems of production. Masters do not buy the labor power of slaves; they buy the slaves themselves. Lords do not buy the labor power of serfs; rather, they enter into a personal relationship with serfs that includes serfs working for lords. That personal relationship is not and does not include the buying/selling of anyone's labor power.

Why, then, does the confused, mistaken notion that capitalism is a market system persist? The answer lies in grasping what this idea accomplishes *when it is believed*.

Defining capitalism in terms of markets—how goods and services are *distributed*—takes attention away from how they are produced. The world of markets can be presented as a place of fairness and equality. In the marketplace, I don't give you something unless I get something satisfying in return. Therefore, a market exchange is a "voluntary" act. Each person is formally equal and free to exchange as they like. These kinds of freedom and fairness can be associated with markets and, thus, with capitalism.

To define capitalism as the employer/employee relationship returns attention to production rather than distribution. In production, the wealth and power of the employer and employee are clearly unequal. One is rich and powerful; the other is not, or at least much less so. Employees do not elect employers. In capitalist workplaces, employers rule; their lack of democratic accountability to the majority, the employees, is obvious. It's far easier to defend capitalism in terms of markets than in terms of production. Hence, defenders prefer the market definition, often to the point of proceeding as if other definitions did not exist.

In this book, I will not refer to capitalism as "the market system," "free market system," "private enterprise system," or "free enterprise system." These labels may defend and distract, but they do not distinguish capitalism from many other systems. As definitions, they fail.

Why Definitions Matter

There's nothing innocent about a definition.

Perhaps you have not heard of the employer/employee definition of capitalism before. If so, that is mostly because capitalism's defenders fear where that definition leads. Not surprisingly, capitalists prefer definitions that better shield their system from criticism.

Over the last few centuries, capitalism's defenders developed many strategies to counter critiques of their system. For example, defenders have attached adjectives to the noun "capitalism" to suggest that any problems or negatives capitalism exhibits reflect some impurity that somehow corrupted an otherwise "perfect" system. Examples of these adjectives include "monopoly," "cutthroat," "imperialist," "vulture," "casino," "crony," "robber baron," and other negatives. When capitalism's defenders admit that such "bad" sorts of capitalism exist, they often insist that they are distortions. A "pure" or "real" or "perfectly competitive" capitalism exists and can be achieved. They often advocate policies for governments to follow that replace "bad" sorts of capitalism with real, pure, competitive perfection.

With the definition of capitalism advanced in this book, problems that arise from capitalism cannot be brushed aside as if they were correctable adjectives. Capitalism's employer/employee core is fundamentally anti-democratic. A tiny group of people—employers—make all the key workplace decisions for a large group of people—employees—and the employees have no say. There is no "fix" for capitalism that removes its anti-democratic qualities and leaves democratic capitalism behind. To democratize capitalist enterprises would be to end their capitalist qualities. In a democratic enterprise, no minority would wield power over a majority: not employers, nor feudal lords, or slave masters.

The employers and fans of capitalism celebrate their system by repeating that it achieved liberty, equality, solidarity, and democracy in society. In practice, capitalism neither achieved those goals nor took responsibility for failing to do so. Some urge us to "get money out of our politics," yet our capitalist economic system not only creates inequality in production but also thereby enables employers to protect their disproportionate wealth by using money to rig the political system in their favor. The undemocratic structure of the employer/employee relationship colonizes our politics to serve capitalism and to reproduce that system.

In capitalism today, we see employers controlling and exploiting employees, a dearth of real democracy, and deep inequality. To those able and willing to see, the similarities and parallels to feudalism and slavery should be arresting.

Current debates about our society's problems and prospects need to refocus. It is time to expose and challenge capitalism's core: the employer/employee organization of enterprises, both private and state. We need to drop the taboo on questioning how we organize the workplaces where most adults spend most of their lives. Workplace organizations affect our lives and shape our societies. A shift away from one form of workplace organization and toward another can help solve social problems and political inequality. To that end, we need to challenge capitalism's workplace organization and escape its constraints on our politics.

Some masters tried to save slavery by promising a different, more compassionate slavery. However, slaves and their allies eventually grasped that the basic problem was not what kind of slavery existed; the problem was slavery itself. Slavery had to end, and debates over its many problems were finally resolved by abolishing the system completely. Likewise, some kings and queens tried to hold to the monarchical system by supporting and crowning more popular kings. Other monarchs allowed parliaments to "advise" them. Eventually, people no longer tolerated the exchange of one kind of monarchy for another; they wanted monarchy's abolition. Capitalism now faces that same historic resolution. Beyond another "reform" of capitalism, its abolition is on the agenda.

Definitions matter more now than ever as people increasingly question and challenge capitalism, seeking to move beyond it. The employer/employee definition of capitalism helps us understand this production system, prepare alternatives, and propose a transition to a genuinely postcapitalist production system. With this definition, we can clearly understand why and in what way we need to change the production system to go beyond capitalism to a better system.

Chapter Three

The Problems of Capitalism

All economic systems have problems. To change from one economic system to another means solving key problems from the first and encountering new problems in the second, some foreseen and foreseeable, others not. During the eighteenth century, it was possible to publicly discuss and debate capitalism's strengths and weaknesses where it was emerging (see especially the writings of Adam Smith and David Ricardo). In the nineteenth century, the discussions and debates intensified as capitalism matured and spread, while also provoking the profound critical response of the socialist traditions (above all via Marx, among many others). However, the quality of debate and discussion changed at the end of the nineteenth and early in the twentieth century. Those were times when socialists based in the employee class became sufficiently numerous and well-organized to challenge capitalist employers for control of governments. Sometimes, the challenges were electoral, while at other times, they were revolutionary.

Once the global struggles of the twentieth century became understood as capitalism versus socialism (chiefly after the Russian Revolution of 1917), public debate and discussion very often deteriorated into lopsided celebrations of one accompanied by denunciations of the other. Debate and discussion gave way to propaganda battles. This happened especially after World War II when the alliance of the US and the Soviet Union collapsed into Cold War opposition. Then propaganda virtually dwarfed serious, careful discussion and debate. Officially, the Cold War ended in 1989, but the taboo on serious discussions of capitalism's strengths and weaknesses—and, likewise, on serious comparisons of those with socialism's strengths and weaknesses—lived on. That taboo extended to a need to represent capitalism and socialism simplistically, as if there were no major variants of capitalism (the US version is not the same as that in Turkey, Germany, Argentina, etc.) and likewise major variants of socialism (the USSR's is not the same as that in Sweden, China, Portugal, or Cuba). See further discussions of these differences in my previous work, "Understanding Socialism." One tragic result of the Cold War taboo is that today, when very serious problems confront and threaten capitalism and also socialism, most people lack the theory, concepts, and facts needed to discuss, understand, and solve those problems. Had we had public discussion without mutually hostile taboos, we would be in far better shape to solve social problems now.

Whether you're a critic of capitalism or one of its loyal defenders, this chapter offers a set of basic problems in capitalism that deserve our attention now. No matter your opinion of capitalism, this chapter will clarify some basic issues and problems the system presents. This part of the book also aims to help you understand growing anti-capitalist feelings around the globe as you think and rethink your own opinions about capitalism and socialism.

We call the topics below problems of capitalism because so few of capitalism's champions (whether politicians, mass media, or academics) admit them. Naming these problems is a kind of medicine to cure our excessive distraction from facing, examining, and trying to overcome them. Large sections of contemporary capitalism are in crisis and decline. Excessive distraction now is especially unwise, undesirable, and dangerous.

Undemocratic

Fans of capitalism like to say it is democratic or that it supports democracy. Some have stretched so far as to literally equate capitalism with democracy, using the terms interchangeably. No matter how many times that is repeated, it is simply not true and never was. Indeed, it is much more accurate to say that capitalism and democracy are opposites. To see why, you have only to look at capitalism as a production system where employees enter into a relationship with employers, where a few people are the boss, and most people simply work doing what they are told to do. That relationship is not democratic; it is autocratic.

When you cross the threshold into a workplace (a factory, an office, a store), you leave whatever democracy might exist outside. You enter a workplace from which democracy is excluded. Are the majority—the employees—making the decisions that affect their lives? The answer is an unambiguous no. Whoever runs the enterprise in a capitalist system (owner[s] or board of directors) makes all the key decisions: what the enterprise produces, what technology it uses, where production takes place, and what to do with enterprise profits. The employees are excluded from making those decisions but must live with the consequences, which affect them deeply. The employees must either accept the effects of their employers' decisions or quit their jobs to work somewhere else (most likely organized in the same undemocratic way).

The employer is an autocrat within a capitalist enterprise, like a king in a monarchy. Over the past few centuries, monarchies were largely "overthrown" and replaced by representative, electoral "democracies." But kings remained. They merely changed their location and their titles. They moved from political positions in government to economic positions inside capitalist enterprises. Instead of kings, they are called bosses or owners or CEOs. There they sit, atop the capitalist enterprise, exercising many king-like powers, unaccountable to those over whom they reign.

Democracy has been kept out of capitalist enterprise for centuries. Many other institutions in societies where capitalist enterprises prevail—government agencies, universities and colleges, religions, charities, and more—are equally autocratic. Their internal relationships often copy or mirror the employer/employee relationship inside capitalist enterprises. Those institutions try thereby to "function in a businesslike manner."

The anti-democratic organization of capitalist firms also conveys to employees that their input is not genuinely welcomed or sought by their bosses. Employees thus mostly resign themselves to their powerless position relative to the CEO at their workplace. They also expect the same in their relationships with political leaders, the CEOs' counterparts in government. Their inability to participate in running their workplaces trains citizens to presume and accept the same in relation to running their residential communities. Employers become top political officials (and vice versa) in part because they are used to being "in charge." Political parties and government bureaucracies mirror capitalist enterprises by being run autocratically while constantly describing themselves as democratic.

Most adults experience working at least eight hours for five or more days per week in capitalist workplaces, under the power and authority of their employer. The undemocratic reality of the capitalist workplace leaves its complex, multilayered impacts on all who collaborate there, part time and full time. Capitalism's problem with democracy—that the two basically contradict one another—shapes many people's lives. Elon Musk, Jeff Bezos, and the Walton family (Walmart's founders), along with a handful of other major shareholders, decide how to spend hundreds of billions. The decisions of a few hundred billionaires bring economic development, industries, and enterprises to some regions and lead to the economic decline of other regions. The many billions of people affected by those spending decisions are excluded from participatiing in making them. Those countless people lack the economic and social power wielded by a tiny, unelected, obscenely wealthy minority of people. That is the opposite of democracy.

Employers as a class, often led by major shareholders and the CEOs they enrich, also use their wealth to buy (they would prefer to say "donate" to) political parties, candidates, and campaigns. The rich have always understood that universal or even widespread suffrage risks a nonwealthy majority voting to undo society's wealth inequality. So, the rich seek control of existing *forms* of democracy to make sure they do not become a real democracy in the sense of enabling the employee majority to outvote the employer minority.

The enormous surpluses appropriated by "big business" employers—usually corporations—allow them to reward their upper-level executives lavishly. These executives, technically also "employees," use corporate wealth and power to influence politics. Their goals are to reproduce the capitalist system and thus the favors and rewards it gives them. Capitalists and their top employees make the political system depend on their money more than it depends on the people's votes.

How does capitalism make the major political parties and candidates dependent on donations from employers and the rich? Politicians need vast sums of money to win by dominating the media as part of costly campaigns. They find willing donors by supporting policies that benefit capitalism as a whole, or else particular industries, regions, and enterprises. Sometimes, the donors find the politicians. Employers hire lobbyists—people who work full time, all year round, to influence the candidates that get elected. Employers fund "think tanks" to produce and spread reports on every current social issue. The purpose of those reports is to build general support for what the funders want. In these and more ways, employers and those they enrich shape the political system to work for them.

Most employees have no comparable wealth or power. To exert real political power requires massive organization to activate, combine, and mobilize employees so their numbers can add up to real strength. That happens rarely and with great difficulty. Moreover, in the US, the political system has been shaped over the decades to leave only two major parties. *Both of them loudly and proudly endorse and support capitalism.* They collaborate to make it very difficult for (1) any third party to gain a foothold, and (2) for any anti-capitalist political party to emerge. The US endlessly repeats its commitment to maximum freedom of choice for its citizens, but it excludes political parties from that commitment.

Democracy is about "one person, one vote"—the notion that we all have an equal say in the decisions that affect us. That is not what we have now. Going into a voting booth once or twice a year and picking a candidate is a very different level of influence than that of the Rockefeller family or George Soros. When they want to influence people, they use their money. That's not democracy.

In capitalism, democracy is unacceptable because it threatens the unequally distributed wealth of the minority with a majority vote. With or without formal institutions of democracy (such as elections with universal suffrage), capitalism undermines genuine democracy because employers control production, surplus value, and that surplus value's distributions. For capitalism's leaders, democracy is what they say, not what they do.

Unequal

As the French economist Thomas Piketty most recently exposed, capitalism, across time and space, has always tended to produce ever-greater economic inequality (see his book *Capital in the Twenty-First Century*, Cambridge, MA: Harvard University Press, 2014). Oxfam, a global charity, recently reported today's ten richest men together have six times more wealth than the poorest 3.1 billion people on earth. The lack of democracy inside workplaces or enterprises is both a cause and an effect of capitalism's unequal distribution of income and wealth.

Of course, inequality predates capitalism. Powerful feudal lords across Europe had blended autocracy with unequal distributions of wealth on their manorial estates. In fact, the largest and most powerful among the lords—the one named king—was usually also the richest. Although revolts against monarchy eventually retired most kings and queens (one way or another), similarly rich dictators reemerged inside capitalist enterprises as major shareholders and CEOs. Nowadays, their palaces imitate the grandeur of kings' castles. The fortunes of kings and top CEOs are similarly extreme and attract the same kind of envy, adulation, and reverence. They also draw the same criticism. Inequalities that marked the economy, politics, and culture of European feudalism reappeared in capitalism despite the intentions of many who revolted against feudalism. The problem: the employer/employee relationship is far less a break from the master/slave and lord/serf relations of production than capitalism's champions had hoped for, assumed, and promised to secure mass support for their revolutions against slavery and feudalism.

The employer/employee relationship that defines capitalism has created staggering inequality by allowing the employer full control over production's surplus. In the past, inequality provoked references to rich capitalists, variously, as "robber barons" or as "captains of industry" (depending on the public's feelings about them). Today, and in this book, they're referred to as "the rich" or sometimes "the superrich."

Is it true that everyone is free in a capitalist system? The answer depends on what is meant by "free." Compare the freedom of Elon Musk, Jeff Bezos, or other rich capitalists with your freedom. Capitalism distributes some income to you and some to Musk, Bezos, and the other rich capitalists. However, to say that capitalism makes each of you free ignores the reality that capitalism's unequal distribution of wealth makes you unfree relative to Musk, Bezos, and the other rich capitalists.

Freedom was never only about keeping the government from bothering you; it was always also about being able to act, choose, and make a life. To call us all free, to use the same word for everyone, erases the very real differences in our access to resources, opportunities, and choices needed for life. Musk is free to enjoy life, going wherever he likes and doing almost anything you could imagine. He may work but need not. The financial cost of anything he might want or need is totally irrelevant for him. The overwhelming majority of Americans have nothing remotely like such freedom. To say that in capitalism, all are free, like Mr. Bezos is nonsense. His freedom depends on the resources at his disposal. You lack the freedom to undertake all sorts of actions and choices because those resources are not at your disposal.

The freedom of the rich is not just different; their freedom negates the freedom of others. Unequal income and wealth always provoke anxiety among the rich. They fear the envy their wealth excites and invites. To protect their positions as systemically privileged recipients of income and, thus, accumulators of wealth, the rich seek to control both political and cultural institutions. Their goal is to shape politics and culture, to make them celebrate and justify income and wealth inequalities, not to challenge them. Having already discussed politics, we turn now to how the rich shape culture to their benefit.

Unequal access to culture is a feature of capitalism. Culture concerns how people think about all aspects of life—how we learn, make, and communicate meanings about the world. Our culture shapes what we find acceptable, what we enjoy, and what we come to decide needs changing. In European feudalism, access to culture for most serfs was shaped chiefly by what the church taught. In turn, the church carefully structured its interpretation of the Bible and other texts to reinforce feudal rules and traditions. Lords and serfs funded the church to complete the system. In modern capitalism, secular public schools undertake formal education alongside or instead of churches and other private schools. In today's world, school education celebrates and reinforces capitalism. In turn, the state taxes employers and mostly employees to fund public schools and subsidizes private schools (which also charge students).

Writers like Howard Zinn and Leo Huberman have penned histories of the US showing that much of what standard school US history textbooks lacked were accounts of the many class struggles against capitalism. Instead, rags-to-riches stories about people like Horatio Alger were popularized. Examinations of the roots of revolt and rebellion against low wages, bad working conditions, and all manner of hardship imposed on the workers of America, however, were not.

In capitalism, mainstream media sources are themselves mostly organized as capitalist enterprises. They depend on, understand, and support profit maximization as the driving force of their enterprises. Their CEOs can and do make all sorts of definitive decisions about what is aired, how events are interpreted, whose careers blossom, and whose end. CEOs hire and fire, promote and demote. On mainstream radio, TV, and film, we almost never see exciting dramas about anti-capitalist revolutionaries who win the day by successfully persuading employees to join them. Rags-to-capitalist-riches dramas are, in comparison, routine storylines in countless mainstream media productions.

In capitalism, culture is constrained to reinforce that system. Even individuals who privately criticize capitalism learn early in their careers to keep such criticisms private. Periodically, ideological battles can and do break out. If and when they coalesce with anti-capitalist upsurges elsewhere in society, cultural criticism of capitalism has been, and can again be, a powerful revolutionary force for systemic change. That is why defenders of the capitalist system instinctually and ceaselessly shape politics, economics, and culture to reinforce it.

Capitalism has often undermined democracy and equality, because doing so has reinforced and actually strengthened the capitalist organization of the economy. As an example of capitalism's corruption of democracy and equality, we consider the mid-American town of Kalamazoo, Michigan.

As in so many other US cities, Kalamazoo's corporations and its rich have used their wealth and power to become richer and more powerful. By donating to politicians, threatening to take their businesses elsewhere, and hiring better lawyers than the city could afford, the rich reduced the amount of taxes they needed to pay to the local government. The rich funded costly, broadly targeted anti-tax campaigns that found a receptive audience among the already-overtaxed average citizens. Once deprived of the tax revenue from the rich, local politicians either (1) shifted more of the tax burden onto average citizens, (2) cut public services in the short run, and/or (3) borrowed money and thereby risked having to cut public services in the longer run to service city debts. Among those they borrowed from were sometimes the same corporations and the rich whose taxes had been reduced after they funded successful anti-tax campaigns.

Eventually, the city saw an accumulation of resident complaints about steadily cut public services (uncollected garbage, neglected streets, deteriorated schools, etc.), alongside rising taxes and government fees. This litany is familiar in many US cities. Eventually, upper-and middle- income residents started to leave. That worsened the existing set of problems, so even more people left. Then, two of Kalamazoo's wealthiest and most powerful capitalists—William Parfet and William Johnston—developed a solution they promoted to "save our city."

Parfet and Johnston established the "Foundation for Excellence in Kalamazoo." They contributed, according to reports, over $25 million annually to it. Since such foundations usually qualify for tax-exempt status at federal, state, and local levels of government, the two gentlemen's contributions lowered their personal tax bills. More importantly, the two could wield outsize local political influence. They would have much to say about how much their foundation funded which public services in Kalamazoo. In this city, the old democratic notion of everyone paying taxes to share in funding the public well-being was replaced by private charity. Public, reasonably transparent accountability was replaced by the less transparent, murkier foundation activities. Public accountability faded as the private whims of private foundations took over.

What used to be called a "company town" (when a major employer substituted its rule for any democratic town rule) often amounted, in the words of PBS, to "slavery by another name." In their modern form, they appear as "foundation cities." Old company towns were rejected nearly everywhere across US history. But, as the Kalamazoo example shows, they have returned with names changed.

While capitalism's general tendency is toward ever-greater inequality, occasional redistributions of wealth have happened. These moments have come to be called "reforms" and include progressive taxation of income and wealth, welfare entitlements, and minimum wage legislation. Redistributive reforms usually occur when middle-income and poor people stop tolerating deepening inequality. The biggest and most important example in US history was the Great Depression of the 1930s. The New Deal policies of the federal government then drastically reduced the inequality of wealth and income distribution. Yet employers and the rich have never ceased their opposition to new redistributions and their efforts to undo old ones. US politicians learn early in their careers what results when they advocate for redistributive reforms: an avalanche of criticism coupled with shifts of donors to their political opponents. Thus, in the US, after the end of World War II in 1945, the employer class changed the policies of the federal government. Over the past eighty years, most of what the New Deal won was undone.

Corporations and the rich hire accountants skilled in hiding money in foreign and domestic places that evade reporting to the US Internal Revenue Service. Called "tax havens," those hiding places keep funds that remain untouched by tax collectors. In 2013, Oxfam published findings that the trillions stashed away in tax havens could end extreme world poverty—twice over. Yet since the revelation of this shocking statistic, the inequality of wealth and income has become more extreme in nearly every nation on earth. Tax havens persist.

Conflicts over income, wealth distribution, and its redistribution are thus intrinsic to capitalism and always have been. Occasionally they become violent and socially disruptive. They may trigger demands for system change. They may function as catalysts for revolutions.

No "solution" to struggles over income and wealth redistribution in capitalism was ever found. The reason for that is a system that increasingly enriches a small group. The logical response—proposing that income and wealth be distributed more equally in the first place—was usually taboo. It was thus largely ignored. The French revolutionaries of 1789, who promised "liberty, equality, and fraternity" with the transition from feudalism to capitalism, failed. They got that transition, but not equality. Marx explained the failure to achieve the promised equality resulted from capitalism's core structure of employer and employee preventing equality. In Marx's view, inequality is inseparable from capitalism and will persist until the transition to another system.

Unstable

Throughout its history, capitalism has been remarkably unstable. As the National Bureau of Economic Research found, every four to seven years on average, capitalism crashes. Alternative terms for "crash" include "recession," "depression," "cyclical downturn," "crisis," "bubble burst," and more. Sometimes, these sudden downturns in productive activity, employment, and investment are short and shallow. Sometimes, they last many years and hurt the economy badly. Three of the worst were the Great Depression of the 1930s, the so-called Great Recession of 2008–2009, and the 2020 crash aggravated by the COVID-19 pandemic.

Capitalism's instability disrupts millions of households, relationships, careers, educations, and dreams. The downturns cut the tax revenues that enable all levels of government to function—and just when government help is most urgently needed. Capitalist crashes cause normal maintenance of homes, cars, workplaces, and public infrastructure to be neglected or postponed. Unemployed workers use up savings. Rates of alcoholism, divorce, and abuse of family members rise—as do physical and mental health problems in general. Capitalism's instability incurs huge social costs. The scars on lives left by capitalism's constant cyclical downturns run deep.

Capitalism's fan clubs often blame its instability on "outside" forces: natural disasters such as floods, droughts, viral pandemics, or government policies, including wars. The system's fans also often justify crashes as the way capitalism weeds out ineffective, inefficient producers from the otherwise healthy and thriving mass of capitalist enterprises. Political economist Joseph Schumpeter famously admitted that capitalism regularly destroyed jobs, inventories, and whole businesses, but he characterized those capitalist crashes as moments of "creative destruction." They established the conditions necessary for the next upswing of capitalist production and growth.

For most of capitalism's history, crashes were widely accepted as almost "natural" cycles. Capitalists consoled themselves as Schumpeter did by focusing on the light they perceived at the end of the tunnel of unemployment and bankruptcies. Eventually, they realized, the unemployed become sufficiently desperate to take jobs that offered lower wages than they otherwise would have accepted. Bankrupt employers lower their prices far enough to secure buyers in depressed markets. Landlords lower rents to factory, office, and store tenants. Lawyers and accountants lower their fees. As all these costs of doing business thus decline, *eventually* they fall far enough to make production profitable again. Falling wages and prices may incentivize renewed investment in production. The economic downturn can thus turn itself into an upturn.

The real problem lay with *eventually:* how long would it take each time for a downturn to produce an upturn? How long would the employee class tolerate that unemployment? Where would the resultant suffering, frustration, and waiting move that class politically? Economic depressions could lead the victims of capitalism's crashes to make common cause with the system's critics. By the nineteenth century, as labor unions, social movements, and socialist parties grew, their alliances posed serious political risks to the employer class.

Team capitalism usually splits over how best to manage system instability. One side feels confident that employees will be disciplined by periodic crashes. Fearing "hard times" and the damage they inflict, employees will be vulnerable to claims that "we all must go through hard times together, making some sacrifices." Corporate and political leaders will blame external events but never the capitalist system itself. Such external events could be wars, bad government policies/politicians, or natural events like droughts, storms, and pandemics. The crucial point was that the crash was never the employers' fault; they were represented as victims alongside employees.

Capitalism's advocates usually want to keep the government from any direct intervention in the core relationship of employer to employee. For them, capitalism's instability must not open the door to such interventions. They fear that employees might then consider using state power to reduce inequality or even proceed to abolish that core relationship in favor of another.

Capitalism's defenders repeatedly rediscover the "laissez-faire" instinct. Early capitalists had a very strong bias against the state as an existential threat because capitalism was born out of, and against the repressive hostility of, the absolute monarchies of late feudal Europe. They wanted the state to leave capitalists and the capitalist system alone (*laissez-faire* roughly translates as "let it be"). Those early prejudices against the state reappear in later protests against unwanted government interference in the "private market and economy." For them, the appropriate response to economic crises is an insistence that state intervention is unnecessary and only makes economic matters worse. The modern proponents of this approach include, among many others, Friedrich Hayek, Ludwig von Mises, and Milton Friedman.

However, the other side among employers and defenders of capitalism fears that capitalist crashes may cut deeply and last long enough to provoke a turn of the employee class toward socialism. They argue that capitalism's downturns can and should be mitigated and that the government is the necessary agent to accomplish that. Thus, in the midst of the Great Depression of the 1930s, an English economist, John Maynard Keynes, showed how to identify emerging crises, understand their causes and workings, and shape government interventions that could prevent, moderate, or shorten economic downturns.

In Keynes' view, the key government interventions were of two kinds. The first focused on the monetary system: monetary policies shaped the quantity of money in circulation, the terms on which money was borrowed and lent, the interest rate. The second focused on the government's budget, using its taxing and spending activities as a means to prevent, moderate, or shorten economic downturns. "Fiscal policies" referred to those government taxation and spending actions aimed at capitalism's instability problem.

Over the last century, capitalist economies have repeatedly struggled through cyclical crises. Their leaders and economic advisors have debated and then applied what came to be called either "laissez-faire" or "Keynesian" policies. Some have tried combinations of the two. Those who hoped that such policies might end capitalism's instability were disappointed. That instability persists. The crashes of 2008–2009 and 2020–2021 proved that. Indeed, those last two number among the worst in capitalism's history.

Beyond that, the supporters of Keynesianism insist that the application of their policies has, at least sometimes, rendered downturns shallower and shorter than they would have been without those policies. Proponents of laissez-faire make similar claims about times when governments did little or nothing in the face of cyclical downturns. As these two sides debate, the cyclical downturns continue to appear and scar the lives of millions around the globe. In trying merely to "manage" these recessions, the economics profession distracts itself and its audiences from wrestling with the much larger issue. Since instability has shown itself to be systemic, system changes are among the logical solutions that ought to be considered, discussed, and debated.

For the last few years, reliance on Keynesian policies has increased with the size of economies and their crashes. One in particular—manipulation of the quantity of money in circulation—became more important partly because the spread of modern monetary theory (MMT) reduced hesitancy to use this policy (even by the establishment that mostly rejected much of that theory). Huge fiscal deficits were repeatedly monetized as central banks printed money (or created it electronically) to buy government debt as fast as it was created. Government debt thus mushroomed by trillions of dollars annually. At the same time, capitalist downturns starting in 2000 provoked the application of the Keynesian monetary policy of dropping interest rates to record lows, at or even sometimes below 0 percent annually. The results of capitalism's instability thus include huge, historically unprecedented levels of government debt but also, in part because of extremely low interest rates, massive run-ups in corporate and household debt.

In 2000, the US national debt—the federal government's debt accumulated across US history—stood at $5.7 trillion, or 55 percent of US GDP that year. By 2022, the national debt had risen to $30 trillion, or 130 percent of GDP that year. That stunning increase in government indebtedness benefited creditors that included US and foreign government agencies, large corporations, and (mostly) wealthy individuals. What those corporations and individuals save from low taxes, they turn around and lend to the government.

US indebtedness to foreign creditors makes it the world's single largest debtor nation. When interest rates rise (as market phenomena and/or anti-inflationary policy tools), servicing the national debt becomes increasingly costly for the government. Rising government debt levels and rising debt-servicing costs are major drags on the federal budget. Those drags are yet more costs of capitalism's instability.

Instability and debt in US history

For the roughly 150 years before the 1970s, the white American working class had experienced decade after decade of rising real wages. Prices also went up in that time, but wages rose even more. Rising labor productivity made that possible because it also delivered rising profits to capitalists. Because working-class families could afford steadily rising consumption, the period of the 1820s to the 1970s provided most US workers the best-rising standard of living among all capitalist economies. They came to believe that they lived in a uniquely charmed country. For the religious, it was proof God favored the United States. For others, it was proof that capitalism was the "best" economic system. Celebrations of American exceptionalism blunted the appeals of socialism and other criticisms of capitalism.

The long period of rising real wages stopped in the 1970s. The US working class was stunned, perhaps even traumatized. But by that time, socialist movements and impulses in the US had largely been destroyed by McCarthyism and the Cold War. Working-class families were left without explanations or criticisms of how and why US capitalism stopped raising real wages. Those families thus blamed themselves rather than a system that had ceased working for them. They struggled all the more to maintain consumption levels—the size of the house, the number of cars, and the vast array of consumer goods—despite stagnant real wages.

To that end, more members of working-class families entered the paid workforce: primarily women, and secondarily the elderly and teenagers. Family members who were already employed took on more hours of work or a second or third job. American working-class families also used up savings and violated old traditions of thrift and saving money. Pressed also by enormous promotion from the banks, they shouldered rising debt.

The banks hawked "consumer services" consisting of credit cards and direct loans, profitably mining the working-class desire for "the American dream" of a steadily rising standard of living. Since their real wages had stopped rising, they had to borrow to realize that dream. Once again, capitalism found new ways to profit and old ways not to grasp their costs: huge new household debt levels risking bigger crashes, costly bailouts, and so on. That is how capitalism works. We are living through the realization of those risks now.

In this new economic context, when profiteering lenders increasingly pushed mortgages (loans for purchasing a home) onto low-income ("subprime") people in the years before 2008, they set the stage for yet another capitalist crash. It arrived when deteriorating economic conditions undermined many people's ability to make the monthly payments on their mortgage debt. Profiteering mortgage lenders lost revenues, so they, in turn, defaulted to the banks and others from whom they had borrowed. Investors who speculated in securities backed by mortgage loans saw their values collapse. Defaults spread across the entire credit system, wrecking the financial positions of borrowers and lenders alike. Many financial instruments (especially credit default swaps) had been created on the basis, ultimately, of underlying mortgages. The ramifying default triggered financial panic and a major crash we've come to call "the Great Recession" or "the financial meltdown."

Besides the mortgage crisis in 2008, we've had two other downturns in the last twenty years: the dot-com in 2000 and the COVID-19 in 2020. In each of those crises, the desperate anxiety of the government was that the financial panic would deepen into a general economic downturn. In each case, the government directed the United States central bank, the Federal Reserve, to cut interest rates nearly to zero. That made money extremely cheap to borrow. The Federal Reserve lent it to the banks, and the banks lent it to the corporations. This was supposed to stimulate borrowing and flood the economy with cheap money. The Fed hoped that businesses would borrow and produce more by hiring more. That would then prevent, or at least reduce, the risk of a general collapse. In any case, after 2000, the total debt of nonfinancial corporations soared to record levels.

What happens if prolonged economic crises occur and make it difficult for corporations to pay back loans? Typically, they fire people. The money no longer needed for wages of fired workers becomes available instead to pay off debts.

Such tragedies do not occur because capitalists are cruel but because the system works that way. Capitalism gives a tiny group of people—employers—the means and the profit incentive to squeeze workers' wages, get them into debt, and then penalize or bankrupt them when they cannot pay off the debt. Capitalism thus widens the inequality of wealth and income, redistributing them from those who can afford it least to those who already have it. No wonder capitalism's critics view such a system as unjust.

Another element of corporate debt demonstrates capitalism's unstable nature. Zombie corporations are capitalist enterprises whose profits are not enough to pay the interest on their debt. Technically, such businesses are bankrupt—they cannot cover their obligations. To avoid collapse, zombie corporations borrow more money, using it to pay off the interest on their older debts. Of course, then they'll be in even deeper trouble because they now have even more interest to pay on the extra borrowing.

Nearly one out of five capitalist corporations in America is in zombie territory. Why did this happen, and what does it mean? This takes us back to the Federal Reserve. It has so far responded to the crises of the twenty-first century by making money available at close to zero interest rates for many years. Corporations thus found that borrowing nearly costless money was often the cheapest, easiest, and quickest way of dealing with business problems. Alternative solutions (such as changing their product mix or their technology, retraining workers, relocating production, etc.) were less attractive.

Textbook capitalism is not supposed to work this way. If a company cannot cover its expenses, that company's existence should be questioned. Capital should move to another company that is profitable or at least less of a zombie. But if a stagnant company can easily borrow to cover its costs, its continuance slows down the larger economy's growth. If zombies' debts become enormous relative to their underlying businesses, their creditors may balk at further loans. Creditors fear that zombies might declare bankruptcy and never repay accumulated loans. No creditor wants to be stung like that. Some may pull back early to avoid the risk of being late. Bankruptcies dump cascading effects on everyone connected to the doomed zombie.

An otherwise-modest economic downturn of the sort that often afflict capitalism can turn into a major crash if it drives enough zombie corporations over the edge into bankruptcy. Capitalism's vulnerability to the zombie risk reflects the system's internal mechanisms that create and enable zombies in the first place. Capitalism's instability is inherent.

Reactions to instability

Capitalism has so far failed to bring an end to its inherent economic instability. Its periodic cycles create deep insecurities among the system's people and leaders. The system's ups and downs—in unemployment, income, inflation, and government responses to them—shake and sometimes destabilize whole societies. Sooner or later, workers grasp they could lose their jobs, wages, and living situations in one of those recessions that happen on average every four to seven years. When workers understand this as the systemic instability of capitalism, they change from mere victims into critics of the system. Thus, capitalists and their protectors have always needed ways to deflect mass anxieties, protests, and the risks that workers might mobilize to leave capitalism behind altogether.

One way US capitalists found entailed using racism to exempt a majority of workers from the system's instability. US capitalists could secure most white workers' jobs even during economic downturns by imposing much more unemployment on the African American minority. The latter were last hired and first fired. They were effectively assigned the social function of disproportionally absorbing economic downturns. As "shock absorbers" for capitalism's recessions, African Americans were most damagingly impacted by capitalism's cycles. White Americans' jobs and lives were thus disrupted far less often. Racism functions to prevent seeing unemployed African Americans as capitalism's victims.

Racists are those who came to believe that African Americans are unemployed more because they are somehow inherently less productive than their white counterparts. Thus, in their view, capitalism is not the cause of unemployment; rather, race renders African American workers unemployable. Capitalism's defenders claim that Black workers are paid less, fired more often, and denied credit more often because their work is less valuable, their creditworthiness is poor, and so on—all as racial characteristics.

The employment shocks imposed by capitalism's instability on white Americans are basically fewer in number, lesser in frequency, and shorter in duration than those imposed on African Americans. An old adage summarizes this: "When America gets a cold, the black community gets the flu." This adage often extends to other social groups as well—such as women, Hispanic Americans, and Indigenous Americans. White people get relative security from the ravages of the system's instability because it distributes those ravages unequally across the working class. That inequality is then justified in racist, sexist, and parallel modes of discrimination that blame the victims. The well-known statistical inequalities between African Americans and white Americans (in terms of income, wealth, savings, homeownership, geographic stability, political participation, etc.) flow directly from their different relationships to capitalism's instability. Not surprisingly, white Americans have greater sympathy for capitalism.

Handling capitalism's instability in such discriminatory ways has social effects. In the US, white men traditionally save more and more easily than others. They get promoted sooner and further, can afford better homes, cars, and clothes, and can more easily obtain bank loans. In such a stratified system, differences among social groups deepen over time, and with them all sorts of anxieties, fears, and resentments. Racial and gender-based tensions can worsen, especially if people believe intrinsic differences cause and explain different positions in the economy rather than seeing how systemic economic problems—like instability—contribute to turning differences into inequalities and tensions. Capitalist instability has a clear role in and responsibility for its contributions to racial and gender hostilities and discriminations in capitalist societies (a topic explored in greater depth below, in "The Relationships of Capitalism: Capitalism and Racism").

Capitalist instability can become so extreme that it provokes profound and sometimes also violent social changes. The worst, deepest, and longest-lasting cyclical downturn in capitalism's history to date—dubbed the Great Depression—lasted from 1929 to the early 1940s. So severe was unemployment in 1933 that one in every four

US workers was jobless, and around the world, millions moved closer to destitution than ever before. They demanded to know what had brought them to this tragic situation.

In Germany, the Great Depression (1929) hit after the loss of World War I (1918) and a period of mega-inflation (1923) that had wiped out most Germans' life savings. "Why?" was the question of the day. Socialists and communists blamed capitalism, and their ideas generated a large following. At the other end of the political spectrum, politicians like Adolf Hitler built their Nazi Party by blaming Jews and other "bad people," framing them as evil "races" who had somehow ruined Germany. Hitler and the Nazis he led promised to fix the situation. If given government power, they would merge their Nazi Party with the leaders and owners of Germany's major capitalist industries to form a kind of private–state partnership capitalism. Such a merger is a core part of what "fascism" means. German fascism promised it would create jobs in the workplaces it ran with no interference allowed from unions or any other social institutions. Nazis would (and did) destroy all left-wing social movements and organizations. Workers and their families could join only fascist organizations. The Nazis banned or destroyed all other social organizations and communities (including independent unions, church groups, civic associations, political parties, cultural groups).

Hitler justified such repression as necessary to enable fascism to make Germany a great empire again. He likewise required the persecution, imprisonment, and eventually the murder of millions of Jewish people and other groups relentlessly portrayed as enemies of or obstacles to making Germany great again. Fascism, which repeatedly led to such horrors, has been one response to capitalism's instability. (For more on this topic, see "The Relationships of Capitalism: Capitalism and Fascism" below.)

In the US, the crash and Great Depression provoked a few fascist movements but, much more prominently, also a major political shift to the left. Where Nazi fascists arrested and assassinated unionists, socialists, and communists in Germany, the American government of Franklin D. Roosevelt worked with existing unions and their leaders, as well as socialist and communist parties. These differences in reactions to capitalism's great crash culminated in World War II, where the US allied with the Soviet Union to defeat Hitler, Benito Mussolini, and their jointly championed fascism.

Sometimes called "state capitalism of the left," FDR's response to capitalism's great crash entailed a huge increase in the size and range of government interference in the private sector. Laissez-faire was brushed aside as policy and replaced by what might also be called "extreme Keynesianism." Washington regulated the capitalist economy by such measures as mandating a legal minimum wage, raising taxes on corporations and the rich by record amounts, imposing regulations on markets, substituting state-run rationing for markets in a long list of commodities, and establishing a state pension system (Social Security), a state unemployment compensation program, and more.

Capitalism's Great Depression weakened the forces favoring laissez-faire government policies inherited from capitalism's pre-crash past. At the same time, that depression strengthened support for Keynesian economics in the US and globally. To many people, what Keynes advocated for and what the Soviet Union had already established—despite many other differences between them—were kinds of state capitalist economies that had much in common. It is thus no wonder that pro-laissez-faire lovers of capitalism used the epithet of "socialism" simplistically to label Keynesianism as somehow connected, Cold War style, to a demonized Soviet Union.

Of course, Keynesianism—like capitalism, socialism, and most other large social movements and institutions—takes multiple forms that vary from one another. Differing social and historical contexts shape how theories and practices get interpreted, applied, and adjusted in different places and times. Keynesian economic policy differs from one nation to the next. Similarly, Saudi Arabian capitalism today is different from US capitalism. Swedish socialism is different from Soviet socialism. The Keynesian economic policies that Hitler used are different from those FDR used or those many current leaders use. Intense debates among capitalism's defenders have always reflected, underscored, and often deepened their different understandings of economics and their different interpretations of theories and policies. The same applies to debates among advocates of socialism.

Capitalism's cyclical crashes have provoked debates over how best to prevent or overcome them. From capitalism's inception, that instability often victimized people, some of whom became system critics. Some went further, organizing social movements opposed to capitalism's particular distributions of wealth, its interactions with the natural environment, its extensions into colonialism, and countless other issues. Others targeted particular forms of capitalism (such as laissez-faire or Keynesian state capitalism). Still others went beyond which aspects and forms of capitalism to favor, fighting instead for a social transition to a fundamentally new system. In these debates, discussions, and conflicts, words like "socialist" and "capitalist" took on multiple, different, and evolving meanings. Today's many concepts of capitalism and socialism are products of capitalism and its critics.

In conclusion, if you lived with a roommate as unstable as the capitalist system, you would probably have moved out long ago.

Inefficient

To ask, "Is capitalism efficient?" is immediately to run into trouble. Answers will vary depending on how "efficient" is understood/defined--whether in terms of an employer seeking profit, a consumer seeking utility, or a worker seeking a high standard of living. Or might it be the efficiency of capitalism in providing adequate housing, food, water, and health care to all humanity? Is it efficient in addressing the climate change process that threatens billions of lives? Is capitalism efficient in some ways and not in others?

The fact is that efficiency is a problematic, inadequate, and downright misleading concept to begin with. Moreover, it uses similarly deficient measurements. Yet it is often linked closely to capitalism, because its supporters lean heavily on "efficiency" to justify its existence, effects, and alleged superiority to other economic systems.

In the usual, rough definition used by economists, what happens in an economy—any act or event such as hiring an employee, lowering an interest rate, raising prices, or investing in a factory expansion—is efficient if its total positive consequences ("benefits") exceed its total negative consequences ("costs"). Thus economists measure costs and benefits to see which is larger. If total costs exceed total benefits, the act or event is deemed inefficient and should not happen. If measurements yield the reverse, then the act or event is efficient and should happen. To choose among any two or more events that all have net-positive benefits, the most efficient event is the one with the most benefits compared to its costs.

From the point of view of capitalists, entering a business venture is an act that entails costs (for rent, inputs, wages, etc.), which are its negatives, while the revenues such a business receives are its positives. The larger the excess of total revenues over total costs—that is, profits—the more "efficient" it would be to start that business. Once the business is underway, the same comparison of its total costs and revenues (measured in profits) will determine whether it is an efficient or inefficient business. And the same approach would determine the efficiency (or not) of a decision to sell or close the business.

For centuries, this simple definition crucially supported claims by cheerleaders of capitalism that it is an efficient system. Businesses are established, function, and grow only if and when their business decisions (acts) are generally profitable: when their benefits exceed their costs. Proponents of capitalism have often extended this efficiency calculus to all individuals and the decisions they make. They claim each person decides to pursue an education or take a job based on making a cost-benefit analysis.

Thus, to the extent that the profit motive governs enterprises, capitalism's defenders declare it to be the model efficient economic system. Any interference in economic affairs by employees, the state, or any other institution or social force imposing any decision-making rules other than profit-seeking is denounced. Such interferences impose economic inefficiency on the society in which they occur. It follows, for capitalism's defenders, that any economic system that rejects profit as *the* standard for economic activities will be less efficient than capitalism. Equating capitalism's maximization of profit with economic efficiency is a key defense for capitalism.

Critics have long argued that capitalism's profits flow to employers alone: a minority relative to the employees, who are usually the vast majority within businesses. Profit maximization rewards a minority of those engaged in capitalist enterprises. As explained earlier, profit-seeking capitalist employers usually seek to "save on labor costs" and so tend to lower employees' share of output. Capitalism's profit drive, then, benefits employers at the expense of employees. Such politically effective critiques of capitalism might be refuted if equating profit maximization with efficiency held any water. Unfortunately for capitalism, it does not.

To see through this defense, let's look straight at what efficiency is. It claims to list and then to measure all positive and all negative consequences of some act or event, and to compare them. But if you stop to think about it, that is, in reality, absolutely impossible to do.

For any act or event, the very idea of cause and effect turns out to be very problematic. For each item on a list of positive versus negative consequences, the question must be asked: Is it a consequence of only the one act whose efficiency we are trying to establish? Might several, many, or an infinity of factors cause the consequences on any such list? If so, we cannot link any one effect to any one cause. The event whose efficiency we want to calculate did not alone cause the good or bad outcome; it alone is not responsible for either the benefits or costs. Stated another way, costs and benefits are results of many factors, never of just one. And if every act has many consequences, each of which has many causes, then measuring efficiency of a particular enterprise, event, or action has no meaning.

There are more problems with "efficiency." Many consequences of any act or event whose efficiency we want to assess will not materialize until the future; such consequences cannot be measured now. We cannot know now whether they are positive or negative or by how much. The list of impacts flowing from any act or event is likely very long. It will take time to measure them all, yet we need an efficiency calculation now. Moreover, those impacts are different, affecting the economy but also politics, nature, culture, and so on. How do we reduce qualitatively different consequences to a single monetary value so we can compare more and less, benefits and costs? There is no one or right way to do that, and there never was. It turns out that measuring efficiency in the cost-benefit sense is impossible.

Consider, for example, producing and selling a cup of yogurt. Is that an efficient thing to do? An efficiency analysis would have us weigh its positive impacts (like the consumer's pleasure, the seller's profit, and so on) against its negative impacts (like the resources used up in maintaining cow herds, or in producing, shipping, and refrigerating yogurt). But hold on. The impacts should also include long-term effects. How will yogurt bacteria interact with human gut bacteria over the long run, shaping consumers' health? What is the cost of medical care for those health effects? What about the disruptions to climate associated with the cow herd's methane gas releases? Such lists go on forever.

The fact is that no one has the time, resources, or ability to list all the possible impacts across all of space and time, let alone to measure them in some comparable, quantitative way. Yet, to get a "correct" efficiency statement, we would have to add up positive and negative impacts to get two numbers—total costs versus total benefits. When you consider their limited focus, you can clearly see that all efficiency claims to date are inaccurate, because they could not and did not do what would be necessary for a complete evaluation.

One might legitimately wonder whether anyone ever took the time and spent the money needed to make such immense lists and calculations—and also honestly admitted the many unknowns entailed in them— before deciding whether an act or event should take place. Is efficiency, then, just a fanciful idea made up so it can be claimed and accepted for some purpose, such as justifying capitalism?

Efficiency calculations happen all around us every day. People use them to justify decisions and acts of all kinds. But those calculations could only ever list and measure a very partial, incomplete list of costs and benefits. Actual efficiency evaluations tell us more about the selection biases of the evaluators than about their object's efficiency. The evaluators had to select what they could measure while ignoring or denying the rest but admitting that was and is rare because doing so renders the efficiency claim null and void. That, too, is the result of acknowledging that any act's or event's costs and benefits are never the results only of that act or event. Efficiency is a mirage.

When capitalists (or those they hire) count costs and benefits, they bother to count only those costs for which they actually must pay and only those benefits that accrue to them as revenue. Those are never *all* of the costs and benefits. Consider, for example, a capitalist whose factory smokestacks belch pollutants into the air. The smokestacks intoxicate the air, water, and soil around the factory, incurring all manner of short- and long-term health costs like asthma, cancer, and a variety of diseases for factory employees and people living in the area. Only rarely do the factory-owning capitalists have to pay those costs, so they are not counted when evaluating such a factory's operation. The same applies to benefits that are not profits for the calculating capitalists. Economists refer to such costs and benefits as "external" or "externalities",—which really only means that those costs and benefits are not usually counted.

Let's take the example of this event: a worker is fired. Capitalists fire workers when it isn't profitable to keep them. Every honest capitalist will tell you that. When an employer fires a worker, the employer loses the output that the worker's effort helped produce for the employer to sell. The employer gets fewer widgets than that worker helped to make, or perhaps a lower quality or quantity of a service that the worker produced for the employer to sell. The employer's loss is the cost. The employer's benefit is not having to pay the fired worker any wage. If the wage is greater than the value the worker's labor produced, it advantages the employer to fire the worker. For the employer, the only cost that matters is the lost output of the fired worker.

But the same is definitely not true for the larger society. We know the many real costs of unemployment. Alcoholism, divorce, and abuse in families all rise during unemployment. They require medical care, psychological attention, and police activity; those all cost money. The employer is exempted from paying those costs, but others have to, and do. Society pays all the real costs of unemployment. The employer pays for only a small part of those costs. Yet the employer makes the decision to fire. It is efficient for the employer but extremely inefficient for the society as a whole. Keeping the fired worker on the job and paying a wage is far less costly than what unemployment costs, if and when all the associated costs are considered. The social cost of unemployment exceeds the private cost to the employer, but capitalism allows private employers to decide whether or not to fire. Externalities provide yet another reason to dismiss efficiency claims as bases for defending capitalism.

Worse, externalities show us that social costs are borne by all of us while profits accrue only to capitalists. That is both undemocratic and unfair. Efficiency is an empty concept. It cannot rationally demonstrate that capitalism is superior to socialism or vice versa. To say something is efficient, or more efficient than something else, is the modern equivalent of what ancient people insisted was God's will. To say something was God's will was their attempt to end debate, disagreement, and dispute by appealing to something above our human differences, something absolute that all must recognize as decisive and definite. Eventually, most people became skeptical about anyone's claim to know what God's will was. When will people stop accepting the comparable claims about efficiency?

It is a bit easier nowadays to mock the idea of efficiency because widely held common sense recognizes its limits and problems. The ecological movement has taught this generation that capitalists never counted many of the negative consequences of their investment and production decisions. We now know those threaten not only capitalism but our planet itself.

Capitalism is neither profitable because it is efficient nor efficient because it is profitable. Rather, efficiency became capitalism's preferred code for profitability. It sounded so much better to say that some capitalist's business decision was efficient (good for everybody). To instead say that the same business decision was profitable risked it being seen as good for only the capitalist. Efficiency made a system that was mostly good for a minority (capitalist employers) and often bad for a majority (employees) appear instead to be absolutely and objectively the best for everyone. Equating efficiency to profitability did for capitalism what religion did for European feudalism: it redirected everyone's attention away from the intractable conflict between lord and serf to the unconflicted heavens guided by a God who was all good. Instead of accepting and endorsing capitalism because God tells us to, the economists tell us to do so because capitalism is efficient. Of course, here in the US, we have quite a few folks who will insist that capitalism is both godly and efficient.

Immoral

Morality is among the important standards or measures with which alternative economic systems confront and struggle with one another. In some definitions of morality, some or all outcomes of markets or of capitalist production systems are *moral*. In other definitions, some or all of those outcomes are *immoral*. The debates over the moralities of alternative economic systems often broaden to a debate over morality itself.

Modern capitalism started in England, spreading to Western Europe and then to the rest of the world. It mocked and rejected many of European feudalism's moral commitments. Because medieval Catholic teaching widely held the charging of interest on loans to be sinful, usury was prohibited. The church regulated markets around the concept of what it believed to be the "just" price. For centuries, the church also condemned private property in land as deeply immoral. In contrast, the capitalism that replaced feudalism embraced lending at interest, urged sellers to charge "whatever the market will bear," and made land (and much else) a commodity with no moral taint.

Eventually, the church gave in. Religion adjusted to the transition from feudalism to capitalism by supporting the latter as fully as it had supported the former. Religions accommodated capitalist morality's replacement of feudal morality. Capitalism developed other institutions that articulated and enforced morality alongside the religious institutions: secular schools, mass corporate media, advertising, and so on.

In the drive for profit, capitalist enterprises often found themselves producing more than markets could absorb. To persuade people to purchase more goods and services, modern capitalism created the advertising industry. Advertisers' clients—mostly capitalist employers—pay them to promote those clients' produced goods and services to potential buyers. Advertisements invade every corner of capitalist societies with carefully crafted messages that deeply affect our sense and definitions of morality. Real and imaginary *positive* qualities of every advertised product are stressed repeatedly. Negative qualities of every advertised product are minimized or hidden. Instead of discussions about objects that evaluate their good and bad qualities to create a balanced assessment, advertising hammers at us a model of discourse that is systematically dishonest. Exaggeration slides into lying, and both settle into social life as obvious, routine, and largely accepted parts of modern culture. Morality accommodates.

The ways capitalism uses technological progress entail immorality as well. For example, imagine a new machine that is twice as productive as an old one. Typically, a capitalist employer fires half the employees, produces the same output as before (thanks to the newly installed machine), charges the same price, and thus earns the same revenue. This employer's profit, however, has risen by the amount of wages no longer paid to the fired workers. Those saved wages become the employer's profit. The fired workers and their families suffer the lost wages, and their communities suffer the secondary effects of the workers' lost wages. In capitalism, the employer is not held responsible for having installed new technology in a manner that caused such suffering. If existing definitions of what is moral include caring for other human beings and minimizing others' suffering, then immorality is built into capitalism's core structure. Or the definition of morality must be radically altered.

The immorality of this employer's profit-driven behavior resides in the neglect of the alternative mode of installing the new technology: the employer could have fired *no* workers and still taken full advantage of the new machine by cutting all workers' labor time in half and yet paying them the same wage. That would keep output the same as before the new technology, and likewise—with price and total revenue unchanged—the employer's profit would be the same as before the new machine was installed. The technical change had the potential to revolutionize the lives of the employees (the workplace's majority) by converting half their work time into leisure (time for relationships, art, sport, etc.). That potential is usually ignored, while profit maximization is treated as the appropriate step to take. Yet the choice between these alternative ways of installing new technology has a clear moral dimension. Ignoring the moral choice does not mean it disappears. Many conventional moralities would have to find that capitalism often uses technology in immoral ways.

Critics of markets have denounced their immorality for many centuries, since well before modern capitalism. Markets allocate whatever is scarce—whatever generates demand that is higher than its supply—to the bidder offering the highest price (likely among the richer buyers). Most moral systems would not endorse distributing scarce goods that way. They would rather offer other criteria for allocating scarcities, such as buyers' different needs, community needs, or possible combinations of these.

President Franklin D. Roosevelt instituted rationing in the early 1940s to prevent market immorality from controlling the United States during World War II. His logic held that during wartime—when consumer goods were scarce because resources had been shifted to producing military goods—letting the market govern consumer goods' scarcity would be immoral. The rich would bid up the prices of what they wanted among scarce consumer goods, while those with middle and low incomes would be unable to afford those higher prices. A wealthy family could pay more for milk to feed a pet cat. Meanwhile, a poor family couldn't afford the higher-priced milk for their children. The market handles scarcities, no matter their particular causes or origins, by favoring the richest over everyone else. To say the least, there are moral problems with doing that. FDR suspended the market and substituted rationing across the US. Scarcities were handled by distributions based on need, not on the relative wealth of buyers.

Scarce taxicab rides, scarce preschools, scarce sporting-event tickets, scarce restaurant tables: such goods are often handled by markets in the same immoral manner. They go to those able and willing to pay the much-higher-than-usual prices charged for them. Sometimes, laws render it illegal to charge more than the usual or cost-determined or regulated price when scarcity occurs. However, even then, higher prices occur often "under the table."

Another example, pertinent to contemporary history, can illustrate capitalism's structural immorality. Rising prices—or "inflations"—are another regular part of capitalism, recurring from time to time and place to place across the world. An inflation happens if and when employers in general (not necessarily everyone) raise the prices they charge for whatever goods and services they sell. The immediate cause of inflations then, is employers raising their prices. This will damage employees' real incomes unless they can raise their money wages at rates equal to or more than the rate of inflation. This employees rarely manage to do. Typically, prices rise more than wages. If so, employers gain and employees lose. A minority unaccountable to the majority can and does take actions that directly damage the ma-jority. In a context where democracy is considered a moral imperative, inflation is thus immoral. That immorality is then magnified when we consider that inflations usually present all potential buyers with the same raised prices, and that those are more burdensome for the poorer than the richer. The US and Europe experienced a general, serious inflation after 2020. Of course, a morality that equates market outcomes with the good would not find these results of inflation to be a moral problem.

Particular industries can likewise experience inflations even if and when the rest of the economies surrounding those industries experience none, or different rates of inflation. Sometimes we have developed special words for inflations in particular industries. For example, the word "gentrification" refers to an inflation in housing (houses and/or apartments).

Gentrification is a market phenomenon. Landlords are constantly trying to get more money out of their properties by raising the rent or the price of a home. When prices rise, those who cannot afford the higher prices usually start looking at properties just outside that neighborhood. In the nearby neighborhoods, landlords can then decide to raise their prices as well. The process often repeats itself; gentrification expands. Neighborhoods change as prices rise. Stores and restaurants geared to the poorer people who were there before (often for decades) go out of business or move. "Upscale" or "higher-end" stores and restaurants replace them.

Gentrification is how the market in housing works. Where morality enters the picture is when we ask what happens to the former inhabitants of the now-gentrified homes. Why were they forced to leave their neighborhood? How is a family's life disrupted when they have to leave their old home, neighbors, and schools? Few recognize the question; fewer still worry about the answer. In practice, the victims of gentrification are ignored or, if they protest, probably repressed. In the US, private landlords have mostly succeeded in preventing public housing from competing with private housing. Conventional morality recoils at the spectacle of how capitalist markets "manage" the US housing system. Morality that has fully accommodated itself to capitalism does not.

Instead of diverse communities, housing markets and gentrification produce uniform areas and neighborhoods segregated along lines of wealth (and, therefore, race). The gentrifier often complains: I moved into a vibrant, old, diverse community for just those qualities, but as the gentrification proceeded, all those qualities vanished, and a stale, richer uniformity took over. If our nation could discuss, debate, and make a democratic decision on what kinds of neighborhoods we wish to live in, different moral sensibilities might play a role in the final decision. Instead, "let the market decide" covers for the reality that markets let the rich decide.

No morality is universal. But in this book, it is our view that market outcomes are frequently immoral when they force people to move against their will or distribute basic necessities to the highest bidder.

In relation to morality, consider also the simple structure of capitalist enterprises. A tiny number of persons at the top—owner, partners, corporate board of directors—make all the basic workplace decisions and wield dominant power. If morality—as derived from religious or other ethical systems—requires treating others as human beings in a relationship of basic human equivalence, capitalism violates that morality in its workplaces, where most adults in society spend most of their lives.

Out of competition for ever-greater sources of labor, resources, and markets, capitalism's old centers (Europe, North America, and Japan) have spent much of their history colonizing vast portions of the rest of the world. Colonialism often began with massive violence (sometimes genocidal) perpetrated against populations, and it required ongoing violence to protect and operate the colonies. The moral implications of such a process go without saying. Colonies themselves also suffered as subordinate entities to the colonizing countries' economies. Land, people, and natural resources of colonies were reorganized with enormous losses of lives and cultures. After state independence was established for many colonized countries, neocolonialism functioned in the same way.

Liberty, equality, fraternity, democracy, and most other measures of morality played secondary if any roles in what was done in and to colonies.

To the extent capitalism today contradicts those values, it also contradicts morality. To the extent that future systems challenge capitalism in the years ahead, concerns about morality will animate such challenges.

Self-Destructive

The seeds of capitalism's self-destruction are always present. In order to persist through time, capitalism's defining employer/employee relationship both requires and shapes the processes of profit maximization, competition among employers, economic growth, technical progress, and other mechanisms in the economy. However, all those processes have side effects. They often undermine capitalism, block its success, and lay the groundwork for its undoing. Let's take a few examples.

Employers buy and install machines in their factories, offices, and stores when the machines are more profitable than the workers they replace. Having lost their jobs, the replaced workers lose their wages. With less or no wages, the workers can no longer purchase the products that capitalist employers seek to sell. Unsold products undermine an employer's profits, just as the newly installed technology was supposed to raise profits.

Competition among employers can lead them to improve products' qualities as a way to attract business, boost profits, and grow. However, competition can likewise lead employers to cut corners, such as by substituting cheaper, lower-quality inputs, in ways customers may eventually identify and reject, thereby depressing the employers' revenue and profits.

Karl Marx called such features of capitalism the system's "contradictions." He showed how the tensions among capitalism's processes, pushing and pulling (often in opposite directions), gave everything in the capitalist system its particular movement and ways of changing over time. For example, whether profits rose or fell depended on all the processes influencing profits in society. Each process partly strengthens profits and partly undermines them. What finally determines whether profits rise or fall at any moment depends on all the processes of the whole society. All of them together will create a final net effect: the actual profits we find.

The term "overdetermination" was used by Marxist philosopher Louis Althusser to summarize three basic, interconnected ideas: (1) that every process that makes up a society influences every other, (2) that every process is pushed and pulled in different ways and directions by all the other processes overdetermining it, and (3) every process thus exists in contradiction and change. Each part of a society overdetermines and is overdetermined by all the other parts of that society.

Another way to say this is that capitalism—like everything else—is always contradictory and always changing. To understand something means always to grasp its contradictions, the good opposite its bad parts, and their resulting movement. To grasp only one or the other side is to be precisely one sided. Whatever contradictory conditions or qualities we find in anything—like the changes in it—are the results of its overdetermination.

Capitalism is one such set of overdetermined processes existing in change. Each of its constitutive processes is uniquely overdetermined, changing in its particular way.

Marx described capitalism as a complexity whose parts "develop unevenly." Each part of capitalism is uniquely overdetermined by both the other parts of capitalism and all the other processes comprising capitalism's social and natural environment. It follows that capitalism's reproduction in time and place depends on how its overdeterminants are changing and thereby changing their impacts upon capitalism's processes.

Let's suppose the process of selling the outputs of capitalist enterprises is overdetermined in a way that threatens capitalism. For example, a change in customers' tastes makes them stop buying a particular dyed fabric from a group of producers. Capitalist producers of that dyed fabric are threatened with the death of their enterprises if their sales stop. If someone can come up with another social process to offset the former buyers' changed tastes, the threatened fabric makers can be saved. So, someone invents the advertising industry, which finds ways to publicly associate that particular dyed fabric with being attractive to potential lovers. The threatened fabric makers then distribute a portion of their revenues to advertising corporations as payment for producing and distributing such advertisements. The ads change fabric tastes and revive dyed-fabric sales.

The changed fabric tastes changed capitalism by adding an advertising industry. A changed capitalism with a new advertising industry will provoke other firms and industries to purchase advertising. An industry that communicates by telling the public all the good things about a client's product while hiding all the negative qualities has complex social effects. For example, it spreads its type of discourse into personal, family, and work relationships. Instead of thinking and speaking about the balance of positive and negative aspects of and in all those relationships, people think more in the style of advertising. They see positives or negatives rather than unities of both. That changes those relationships in particular ways that react back upon and change capitalism, possibly threatening it in more ways than taste changes ever could.

For another example: capitalism's profit drive has relocated its dynamic center from one to another place across its history. From England, capitalism's dynamic center moved partly to Western Europe and partly to the US to exploit their labor power and resources for greater profits. Within the US, capitalism's dynamic center moved from New England to the Midwest, then to California, in search of capital-friendly government, resources, and land. In more recent decades, capitalism's dynamic centers relocated to China, India, Brazil, and the global South more generally for their cheaper labor and to escape organized labor in the US and Europe. Capitalism's relocations unraveled the British Empire, are now unraveling the US', and may enable a new Chinese empire. Growing social difficulties in all the areas that capitalism relocated away from raise the question: Might capitalism's profit-driven relocations be the early stages of actualizing its self-destruction? Unintended consequences always follow from change because they multiply through the endless links of overdetermination.

Using an overdeterminist approach to capitalism finds, explores, and evaluates its strengths and weaknesses, its growing and declining elements, and how its larger environment (social and natural) supports and yet also undermines it. Like a good doctor assessing our body, a thorough evaluation takes into account the contradictions overdetermined in our body by our body's environment, its interacting parts, and the connections between them. No single medical test suffices to measure and evaluate something as complex as a human body. A good doctor needs multiple diagnostic tests (blood, X-ray, MRI) to "get a picture" of the influences, reactions, and processes that comprise anyone's "health." A doctor using an overdeterminist approach (self-consciously or not) knows and admits that such a picture is always partial as well as changing.

In human history, each economic system is usually born out of a previous system in decline. Given its overdetermination, each system changes; it evolves and develops. Since different economic systems usually coexist, they change internally but also change one another. Eventually, each changing system begins a decline, out of which new economic systems are born. In this precise sense, all systems eventually self-destruct. There is no reason to think capitalism is any different.

When the self-destructive elements in a system get strained to the point of threatening its continuation, the question becomes: Can the system change to overcome the strain, or will it collapse? One way or another, economic systems persist until they no longer can.

Capitalism's capacity for self-destruction has achieved widespread understanding now via the global movements around the issues of climate change and environmental degradation. For centuries, apologists for capitalism have assured us that inequality can be managed if the system grows. An ever-larger pie allows everybody to be satisfied with their increase in consumption without a contested redistribution. And yet, environmentalism shows that perpetual growth threatens our natural environment and thus our survival. No growth or de-growth ideas make battles over redistribution of the wealth produced in capitalist economies necessary for our survival. As was always true, in those battles over contradictions lurks the potential for systemic self-destruction.

It has become almost commonplace (although still hotly opposed by vested interests, right-wing ideological warriors, and others) to see inside capitalism a growth fetish that threatens not only capitalism's survival but that of our species. What many economists disrespected by using the term "externalities" includes the many, many unacknowledged, unmeasured, and yet deeply dangerous side effects of capitalism upon our natural environment. Those externalities undermine the efficiency claims used to justify capitalism. More importantly, environmental costs reinforce the need to explore—more than has yet been done—the tendencies toward self-destruction built into capitalism. As the philosopher G.W. F. Hegel might have said and as his student Marx explained: self-destruction has always been "the other side" of capitalism's creative capacities.

Chapter Four

The Myths of Capitalism

From its beginnings, the capitalist economic system produced both critics and celebrants, those who felt victimized and those who felt blessed. Where victims and critics developed analyses, demands, and proposals for change, beneficiaries and celebrants developed alternative discourses defending the system.

Certain kinds of argument proved widely effective against capitalism's critics and in obtaining mass support. These became capitalism's basic supportive myths.

Capitalism Created Prosperity and Reduced Poverty

Capitalists and their biggest fans have long argued that the system is an engine of wealth creation. Capitalism's early boosters, such as Adam Smith and David Ricardo, and likewise capitalism's early critics such as Karl Marx, recognized that fact. Capitalism is a system built to grow.

Because of market competition among capitalist employers, "growing the business" is necessary, most of the time, for it to survive. Capitalism is a system driven to grow wealth, but wealth creation is not unique to capitalism. The idea that only capitalism creates wealth or that it does so more than other systems is a myth.

What else causes wealth production? There are a whole host of other contributors to wealth. It's never only the economic system: whether capitalist or feudal or slave or socialist. Wealth creation depends on all kinds of circumstances in history (such as raw materials, weather, or inventions) that determine if and how fast wealth is created. All of those factors play roles alongside that of the particular economic system in place.

When the USSR imploded in 1989, some claimed that capitalism had "defeated" its only real competitor—socialism—proving that capitalism was the greatest-possible creator of wealth. The "end of history" had been reached, at least in relation to economic systems. Once and for all, nothing better than capitalism could be imagined, let alone achieved.

The myth here is a common mistake and grossly overused. While wealth was created in significant quantities over the last few centuries *as* capitalism spread globally, that does not prove it was capitalism that *caused* the growth in wealth. Maybe wealth grew despite capitalism. Maybe it would have grown faster with some other system. Evidence for that possibility includes (1) the fact that the fastest economic growth (as measured by GDP) in the twentieth century was that achieved by the USSR, and (2) the fact that the fastest growth in wealth in the twenty-first century so far is that of the People's Republic of China. Both of those societies rejected capitalism and proudly defined themselves as socialist.

Another version of this myth, especially popular in recent years, claims capitalism deserves credit for bringing many millions up out of poverty over the last two to three hundred years. In this story, capitalism's wealth creation brought everyone a higher standard of living with better food, wages, job conditions, medicine and health care, education, and scientific advancements. Capitalism supposedly gave huge gifts to the poorest among us and deserves our applause for such magnificent social contributions.

The problem with this myth is like that with the wealth-creation myth discussed above. Just because millions escaped poverty during capitalism's global spread does not prove that capitalism is the reason for this change. Alternative systems could have enabled escape from poverty during the same period of time, or for more people sooner, because they organized production and distribution differently.

Capitalism's profit focus has often held back the distribution of products to drive up their prices and, therefore, profits. Patents and trademarks of profit-seeking businesses effectively slow the distribution of all sorts of products. We cannot know whether capitalism's incentive effects outweigh its slowing effects. Claims that, overall, capitalism promotes rather than slows progress are pure ideological assertions. Different economic systems—capitalism included—promote and delay development in different ways at different speeds in their different parts.

Capitalists and their supporters have almost always opposed measures designed to lessen or eliminate poverty. They blocked minimum wage laws often for many years, and when such laws were passed, they blocked raising the minimums (as they have done in the US since 2009). Capitalists similarly opposed laws outlawing or limiting child labor, reducing the length of the working day, providing unemployment compensation, establishing government pension systems such as Social Security, providing a national health insurance system, challenging gender and racial discrimination against women and people of color, or providing universal basic income. Capitalists have led opposition to progressive tax systems, occupational safety and health systems, and free universal education from preschool through university. Capitalists have opposed unions for the last 150 years and likewise restricted collective bargaining for large classes of workers. They have opposed socialist, communist, and anarchist organizations aimed at organizing the poor to demand relief from poverty.

The truth is this: to the extent that poverty has been reduced, it has happened *despite* the opposition of capitalists. To credit capitalists and capitalism for the reduction in global poverty is to invert the truth. When capitalists try to take credit for the poverty reduction that was achieved against their efforts, they count on their audiences not knowing the history of fighting poverty in capitalism.

Recent claims that capitalism overcame poverty are often based on misinterpretations of certain data. For example, the United Nations defines poverty as an income of under $1.97 per day. The number of poor people living on under $1.97 per day has decreased markedly in the last century. But one country, China—the world's largest by population—has experienced one of the greatest escapes from poverty in the world in the last century, and therefore, has an outsized influence on all totals. Given China's huge influence on poverty measures, one could claim that reduced global poverty in recent decades results from an economic system that insists it is *not* capitalist but rather socialist.

Economic systems are eventually evaluated according to how well or not they serve the society in which they exist. How each system organizes production and distribution of goods and services determines how well it meets its population's basic needs for health, safety, sufficient food, clothing, shelter, transport, education, and leisure to lead a decent, productive work–life balance. How well is modern capitalism performing in that sense?

Modern capitalism has now accumulated around a hundred individuals in the world who together own more wealth than the bottom half of this planet's population (over 3.5 billion people). Those hundred richest people's financial decisions have as much influence over how the world's resources are used as the financial decisions of 3.5 billion, the poorest half of this planet's population. That is why the poor die early in a world of modern medicine, suffer from diseases that we know how to cure, starve when we produce more than enough food, lack education when we have plenty of teachers, and experience so much more tragedy. Is this what reducing poverty looks like?

Crediting capitalism for poverty reduction is another myth. Poverty was reduced by the poor's struggle against a poverty reproduced systemically by capitalism and capitalists. Moreover, the poor's battles were often aided by militant working-class organizations, including pointedly anti-capitalist organizations.

Monopoly, Not Capitalism, Is the Problem.

Defenders of modern capitalism have often presented it as built on a bedrock of competition. They describe capitalism as *competitive*—understood as a market system in which there are many buyers and sellers of everything, so no one of them has the power to shape any price. Suppliers are said to respond—in terms of the quantities produced and their market prices—to what people want and demand. Every capitalist's profits depend on the market prices of whatever they sell. Workers do not accept wages that are below market averages, because they are free to work elsewhere for higher wages. They likewise demand and obtain the lowest-possible prices by forsaking sellers who charge above the basic costs of production. Competition disciplines all the sellers into charging the lowest-possible price. Competition thus assures that prices and wages reflect both the best that suppliers can produce, and the optimum benefit buyers can obtain from their purchases.

The myth here is the idea that such a capitalism, if it ever existed, could persist. In actuality, where and when competition exists, it self-destructs, thereby reducing the perfectly harmonious market to a mere myth, not a reality.

The goal of competition is to end the competition: *somebody wins*. Winners gain market share, and losers are driven out of business. The failed businesses sell the equipment they no longer need at sale prices to winners still in the business. Former employees of firms who went out of business often find new jobs with the competitive winners. In short, competition turns the many sellers into fewer firms until few or only one is left. When a few businesses dominate the market, economists call that an *oligopoly*. It can survive if those few take steps to stop competition among themselves. If one seller outcompetes the others and becomes the only seller in the market for some product, the winning seller—called a *monopolist*—is able to dictate the price to all potential buyers.

A monopoly firm can wield supreme market power. Monopolies can raise prices (and their profits) above competitive levels because they alone control the supply. Most monopolists do; that's why competitive markets self-destruct. They have a built-in incentive for firms to seek monopoly profits by achieving monopoly positions in their markets, and every firm fears that another firm will achieve such a position first. This is why competitors stress growing their firms: to accumulate the maximum profits, which can then be used to temporarily absorb lowered prices used in the race toward oligopoly or monopoly. Capitalism is a system designed to grow and to consolidate its early competitors into oligopolies and monopolies. Forbidding monopolies, or breaking them up into competitors, only drives monopolization underground or restarts a cycle of competition that will yet again self-destruct.

Marx applied Hegel's notion of contradictions in his analysis of monopolies within capitalism. The high profits achieved by oligopolies and monopolies eventually entice new competitors into the market, each seeking a piece of those high profits. In this way, monopoly self-destructs in favor of competition. Dozens of automobile companies in the US shrank to an oligopoly of three—Ford, GM, and Chrysler—before those three attracted new, foreign competitors (Toyota, VW, and many more nowadays). The variety of cars in the US illustrates how competition negates monopoly just as monopoly negates competition. Of course, competitors and oligopolists/monopolists can approach governments to erect all sorts of barriers to slow or stop movement in either direction. Then, the struggle becomes political as well as economic.

Myth enters the analysis when capitalism's supporters treat oligopoly and monopoly as if they were not intrinsic phases of an inherently contradictory capitalism. Defenders of this system portray oligopoly and monopoly as antithetical, foreign elements that distort the competition of capitalism. They say monopolies render capitalism imperfect and impure (their words). These defenders often *do* admit many of the criticisms of capitalism; but attribute them to oligopoly and monopoly. They believe removing the oligopolistic and monopolistic distortions would leave us with a capitalism that can solve the world's problems and is the best economic system we can achieve.

Policy proposals follow this thinking under the heading of "anti-trust" laws and regulations.

Their mistake is imagining a capitalism without oligopoly, monopoly, or the intrinsic tendencies toward them that every capitalism on record has experienced. This myth invites the demonization of monopolies and oligopolies, and it diverts critical attention from capitalism itself. For example, in 2022–23, critics of raging inflation blamed it on monopolies and their pricing powers (even though the previous twenty years displayed the same monopolization but without inflation). Returning a monopoly capitalism toward a competitive capitalism resumes all the tendencies toward the self-destruction of competition: a policy doomed by its blindness to capitalism's contradictions.

The concept of a pure, perfectly competitive capitalism (without oligopolies and monopolies) is a myth.

Capitalism Is Uniquely Innovative

Champions of capitalism have long argued that it is uniquely innovative: that the profit motive and competition have provoked innovation far more than previous systems could, and that capitalism is far more innovative than socialism could be or has been. However, the notion that capitalism is uniquely and positively innovative is a myth.

First, each economic system contributes to innovations in its own way. Each system promotes innovation in some parts of society more than others, among some people more than others, and around some activities more than others. Innovation in some areas is even stifled or slowed in favor of other areas. In short, the qualities of innovation vary from one economic system to another. Reducing these qualitative differences to a simple measure of quantity—such as more versus less—is a dubious undertaking. How do we quantitatively compare an innovation in woodworking to one in childcare?

What counts as an innovation, and how it is assessed and measured, vary from time to time and from place to place. Nor are the purpose and meaning at all clear of reducing qualitatively different innovations to some homogeneous, simplified quantitative measure of more and less. Capitalism's innovations are different from those of feudalism, slavery, and other systems of the past and likewise different from socialisms of the past, present, and future. Beyond empty boasting, notions of "more" or "less" innovation are myths.

Second, many innovations happening *during* capitalism should not necessarily be *attributed to* capitalism. What about innovations developed despite capitalism: the breakthroughs achieved by an individual after countless corporations had offered only discouragement? Modern computers were partly developed in US universities and by the US military, at least partly because profit-driven capitalists would not take the financial risks involved.

Third, US corporations have repressed certain innovations because they threaten profit. Long-lasting light bulbs mean that fewer get purchased. Planned obsolescence is another gift of capitalism's profit drive in which innovation becomes deliberately wasteful, as the journalist Vance Packard taught many decades ago. Mass public transportation could save many lives, avoid more injuries, save many natural resources, and reduce pollution and dangerous climate change. Instead, driven by the profit incentive, we now replace gasoline-powered private vehicles with electric private vehicles. This is certainly an innovation, but not the one we most need and not the change from which we might well benefit far more.

Fourth, employees in capitalism have often repressed innovations because they led to machines that threatened workers with unemployment.

Finally, profits have incentivized innovations society now sees as partially or wholly destructive, such as burning coal or nuclear reactions to generate electricity, cigarettes, alcohol, synthetic opioids, asbestos, round-up fertilizer and many, many more.

Knowing all the innovations, good and bad, occurring in any one society in any one period is exceedingly difficult. Measuring it would be even more so, as would be measuring those innovations that were repressed. Comparisons of different societies' or historical periods' innovativeness have not been persuasive. Yet capitalism's defenders' claims linking capitalism to innovation persist because they believe them to be persuasively effective.

Human beings interacting with one another and with the rest of nature have always been innovative. People have always recognized problems, obstacles, and opportunities in their lives and responded to them with new ways of doing things—innovations—across all realms of human activity (economic, political, cultural, or personal). They have often wanted to communicate their innovations to one another and across generations and have even innovated to do just that.

Cold War politics required as many ridiculously lopsided comparisons as possible between capitalism and socialism. One was good, and the other bad. Innovation, a good thing, was attributed to capitalism and then contrasted with its absence, a bad thing, attributed to socialism. The idea that "anyone can start a business and innovate under the spur of competition" was said to be true of capitalism but not of socialism. Yet the USSR, for example, exhibited much small business formation on its collective farms, in its service sector, and in its black markets, all replete with competition and innovations. Its defense industries, among others, have good reputations for innovation to this day. The People's Republic of China today enjoys a global reputation for all sorts of innovations in its society, especially in hi-tech sectors competing with the US. Indeed, pre-capitalist economic systems – such as ancient Greece, Rome, and medieval Europe - made major breakthroughs in agriculture, industry, warfare, governance, and other crucial parts of social life. Each was different, but the assertion that capitalism was innovative while other systems were less so is mere ideological self-promotion.

The notion that capitalism is somehow more innovative is a myth.

Markets Are a Neutral, Efficient Way to Distribute Goods and Services

"Market mechanisms" and "market solutions": politicians, bureaucrats, media pundits, and academics like to refer to them as if they were somehow uniquely fair and optimally efficient, which they are not.

The problems with the market system of distribution appear immediately if the demand for an item is higher than its supply in the market. Buyers compete for the item in short supply by bidding up its price. As prices rise for such goods or services in short supply, the poorer buyers drop from the bidding because they cannot afford the higher prices. Eventually, the price stabilizes at whatever higher level equated the demand to the supply. When demand is less than supply, the reverse happens, and prices drop.

Thus, markets distribute items in relatively short supply in a manner that discriminates against those with little or no wealth relative to the rich. Markets are in no way neutral to or "above" conflicts between rich and poor. Of course, sellers could choose not to accept the higher prices some buyers offer and instead produce or order more products to sell. They could, in short, choose to respond to short supply by increasing that supply. In free enterprise capitalism, the decision whether to respond to supply shortages by raising prices (inflation) or by increasing production is left to a tiny minority of the population: employers. Employers decide based on what maximizes their profits. The rest of us live with the consequences of employers' profit-driven decisions.

When employers profit from inflating their output prices, free market advocates argue that the rising price is how the market "signals" to producers to manufacture. Their incentive is to tap into the high profits generated by high product prices. However, this "signaling" feature is well known to all employers. If any employers respond to the signals by producing or ordering more to increase the supply, the high prices and profits-per-product will disappear. So, employers often exhibit no rush to produce more. Indeed, employers stuck in competitive markets envy the monopolizing employers and proceed to copy them: that is, by restricting supply to generate higher prices and profits. And, as high prices proliferate through the market system, more and more sellers begin to excuse raising their own prices because their "costs have risen." The rest of us watch this spectacle of employers profitably using one another as excuses for raising prices.

Capitalists long ago learned that they could profit by manipulating both supply and demand. In that way, they could create "shortages" that would enable them to get higher prices. Capitalism created the advertising industry to boost demand above what it might otherwise be. At the same time, each industry organized to control supply (via informal agreements among producers, mergers, oligopolies, monopolies, and cartels). Changes beyond the control of capitalists require them to constantly adjust how they manipulate demand and supply.

Looking for a job is also handled by markets in modern capitalism. If people looking for jobs outnumber the available jobs, employers can lower wages, knowing that desperate people will often take low wages rather than risk no wages. Historically, this process caused a huge backlash, with workers demanding and fighting for legally enforced minimum wages. Employers everywhere fought against minimum wage laws. When, eventually, such laws were won, employers resisted raising the minimum wage—often successfully. For example, the US federal minimum wage rate of $7.25 per hour was kept from rising between 2009 and 2024 (when this book was written). Employers manipulate the supply and demand for labor power to keep down its price (wages) just as they manipulate the supply and demand for output to keep up its price. Employers replace employed workers with machines (automation) and thereby increase the supply of workers looking for jobs. That usually depresses wages. Employers likewise relocate jobs overseas, depriving US workers of jobs and thereby forcing them to swell the supply of US workers looking for jobs just as employers have left to buy labor power overseas. Thus, the reduced demand for and the increased supply of US workers depresses wages. Manipulation of the labor power market in these ways aims to lower wages, just as manipulation of the product market aims to raise prices. Profit drives the capitalist system.

While actual capitalists manipulate demands and supplies, their defenders praise the mythical abstraction of competitive markets that make capitalist economies ideally efficient by equating supplies to demands (as if they were not continuously subject to capitalists' manipulations).

Markets existed long before capitalism, but capitalism, as Karl Marx noted, spread them throughout societies to unprecedented degrees. Capitalism praises markets—and their prices— to levels of ideological intensity that risk approaching absurdity. As R. H. Tawney so brilliantly showed in his *Religion and the Rise of Capitalism*, early European capitalism had to fight hard to displace the notion of a "just" price inherited from the medieval Catholic Church. The "just" price—consistent with God's laws and Christ's teachings as interpreted by the church—often differed from the "market price" of manipulated supplies and demands. To win that fight, preachers of capitalism built a kind of secular religion around markets and their prices, attributing God-like qualities of efficiency and fairness to them. However, as capitalism sinks into ever-deeper trouble, it is time to debunk economic myths as part of finding our way to better institutions and, indeed, to a better system.

Capitalism Enriches Those Who Deserve Riches

There is no evidence that proves the rich ever worked harder than the rest of us. But they would like us to think so. Wealth is mostly about what positions you occupy in the capitalist system. Are you in a place to which riches are distributed or not? Most of the rich in capitalism do not accumulate their wealth because of work they do (hard or otherwise), or from wages or salaries paid for such work. Rather, their incomes flow from the wealth they own, from their positions as propertied. They owe their wealth to the rents, interest, dividends, capital gains, and profits that accrue to the positions they occupy as owners of land, money, shares, and businesses. Capitalism does not care how an individual comes to occupy such positions (by inheritance, theft, financial maneuver, family intrigue, etc.). In capitalism, income flows to the position of wealth owner (no matter who occupies that position or how they got to do so).

UNDERSTANDING CAPITALISM

Able-bodied, noninstitutionalized adult individuals typically earn incomes in capitalism as employees by working. They sell their labor power (the ability to work) to an employer. For most, working secures the great bulk of their income throughout their lives. Any such employee who also owns productive property (i.e., land, cash, shares, etc.) can earn additional income beyond their wages or salaries by permitting employers to use that property in producing goods or services for sale. The problem is most people own little or no productive property beyond their labor power. They rely on performing labor to earn income. They spend that income chiefly to pay for their consumption; most have little, or nothing left to buy productive property. Without significant private property, employees' income is based on selling their labor power.

Rarely do people become rich if they are not rich to start with. The capitalist world over the last several centuries provides the evidence. Occasional rags-to-riches stories of employees who became employers are the much-hyped exceptions that prove the rule. Most working-class people figure that out—even if it takes years for them to see through the employers' smoke screen about how "hard work pays off." Most of the rich inherited wealth or got crucial help from rich people, enabling them to become rich (or richer). Elon Musk, arguably the world's richest individual, came from a family that owned airplanes and emerald mines. Bill Gates's mother was wealthy. Jeff Bezos's parents gave him $245,000 to get Amazon going as an enterprise. Warren Buffett assembled rich partners (including his wealthy businessman and politician father) who gave him money. The rich are mainly owners of significant amounts of property.

The workers whose labor produced the output and thus the revenues do not get the surplus contained within them. Whether they work very hard, just plain hard, or not hard at all is largely irrelevant.

Because they are excluded from distributing the surplus their labor produces, productive workers rarely get any of it. Capitalism gives employers alone the social position of determining to whom to distribute the system's surpluses. As should surprise no one, they distribute it to that small circle of the very rich from whom they mostly come. As we have seen, capitalism further enriches the already rich.

Education doesn't make students rich, either. Students who became rich were those who found their way into capitalist positions receiving large distributions of the surplus, not because of some particular training. As countless young careerists have had to learn the hard, bitter way: in capitalism it matters less *what* you know than *who* you know. What matters is which position within capitalism your friends, family, and associates can help you get relative to the surplus.

The lucky few top executives join the ranks of those already rich from inheritance, from theft, or from poaching on the global South—those areas of the world that capitalism colonized. Top corporate managers include those charged with "growing the enterprise," or "capital accumulation." If successful, a growing capitalist enterprise can further enrich the already rich and add more individuals to those it enriches. The cycle begins again, and the rich become richer by providing employers with access to their private income-generating property.

In these ways, capitalism has become synonymous with ever-greater income and wealth inequality. Sometimes, majorities revolt against the system because of those inequalities. Sometimes, they succeed in getting minor changes (called "reforms") of the system's income distribution. Sometimes, the revolt spreads and deepens. In those rare moments, demands grow beyond reforms of the system to a revolution, a change in the system.

Both reformist and revolutionary demands are rejections of the myth that rich people in capitalism "deserve" their wealth. In place of those myths, reformers, and revolutionaries often grasp that capitalism is a system that allows and incentivizes some to accumulate wealth produced by others. If your grandparents and your parents were not rich, you are likely not rich either. They were, like you are, excluded from distributing the surplus that productive labor yields. Therefore, the resulting surplus distribution kept them from becoming rich and instead made the already rich even richer.

How bitter, then, the chagrin of the formerly rich, those who lost that position in capitalism that had enriched them. Nothing about their personality, acquired wisdom, or artistic creativity can recover their formerly rich status. After losing their private income-generating property, they must sell their labor power—the sad condition of most of their fellow citizens in capitalism. If no employer wishes to purchase their labor power, even that source of income vanishes. The psychological costs of their descent might explain their declines from corporate bigwig to skid row drunk. They blame themselves for losing their wealth.

Blaming one's individuality, however, distracts attention from the profound ways that capitalism determines who is rich and who is not. You are not southern versus northern, outgoing versus inward, tall versus short, happy versus sad, and so on because you "deserve" it. To think that way mistakes an outcome for an origin. You are the way you are because of all that happened to you. What you did or did not do, what choices you did or did not make were only details. Your decisions and acts were small parts of the much larger overdetermination of all that happened to you in your family, household, friendships, school, church, job, marriage, and so on. All that happened to you thus positions you in one or another place within the capitalist economy. And that position determines whether you are rich or not.

To say the rich deserve their status effectively short-circuits all the complex ways and infinite variables that together determine our lives. The rich who claim they deserve their riches need the poor to blame themselves for being poor. Otherwise, the poor might blame the system that assigned them to that position, or they might blame the rich. Fear of those possibilities has always driven the troubled consciences of slave masters, lords of serfs, and employers of employees. Thus, they cultivated and imposed on their societies the myth that inequalities of wealth, income, and power reward individual merit and effort.

No one should be surprised that corporate executives regularly reward themselves richly, even when the corporations they run lose money for years. It was never about results; it was always about position within the capitalist system. Teaching capitalism's victims to blame themselves - the myth of meritocracy - reduces the risk that the employer class will reap the justified rage of the employee class.

Obscene wealth is justified by huge social contributions

Wherever obscenely rich people have existed, they have gone to extreme lengths to protect their wealth and its privileges from the nonwealthy people working for them. Emperors, kings, czars, masters of huge slave plantations, lords of big feudal manors, and major shareholders and top executives of capitalist megacorporations have all secured protection by armed force (security guards, police, judiciaries, military) and/or by controlling politicians. Donations, control of mass media, lobbyists, and bribery "won" the required political decisions. Laws, regulations, school curricula, proclamations, electoral campaigns and, so on, were the means to justify the distributions that enabled extreme wealth and its inevitable counterpart, extreme poverty.

In today's capitalism, one such myth argues that obscene wealth is society's reward for those people who make the most important contributions to social progress. In two currently popular examples, Elon Musk deserves his tens of billions because he contributed the electric car, and Jeff Bezos deserves his tens of billions for bringing us the speedy ordering and delivery of goods. However, there is a serious logical mistake involved in this mythological argument.

We can show this by considering the man who proudly tells visiting guests, "I added that wing of the house myself." The visitors understand the words that are missing: "I purchased the construction services—labor power, knowledge, skill, and materials—that actually produced the home addition."

Yet the Musk and Bezos myths work differently. They want us to believe that they built Tesla and Amazon. Of course, they did not. They purchased the labor power, knowledge, skill, and materials that actually built those corporations. Taken together, the many different people's contributions were indeed considerable: all that went into electricity, computers, design of automobiles, provision of metals and plastics, communication technology, and much else. All Musk's and Bezos's money did was buy all the goods, services, and knowledge those people had accumulated over years. What is wrongly called "Musk's electric car" or "Bezos's delivery services" would have been impossible without all those prior contributions. To reward contributions and contributors justly would entail rewarding them all. But capitalism does not work that way. Typically, it disproportionally rewards the buyer of produced inputs and labor who also sells the final product.

The relevant parallel here is a village battling to escape flooding from a nearby river's impending overflow. A group of villagers gather to dig sand, acquire sandbags, fill them with sand, and then pass them forward from person to person. The last person standing closest to the river—perhaps called Elon—can then pile those bags on the river's bank. The sandbags prevent a catastrophe, and the village is saved. The villagers collect $10,000 to show their gratitude and give the money to Elon. Rewarding an individual at the end of the line rather than sharing the reward among all those who collaborated to produce the outcome is unjust. It also incentivizes individual self-aggrandizement over teamwork when the community is far better served by teamwork. If contributors to the anti-flood effort had competed for Elon's individual position, disrupting or delaying the team effort, the village might have been washed away, and no reward would have been offered at all. The village would have done better to distribute the collected $10,000 to reward all villagers who collaborated in preventing the flood.

People may try to justify extreme wealth by pointing to the philanthropy that some extremely wealthy individuals sometimes choose to perform. Look at what good they are doing! Surely, they are being responsible with the wealth they have, and therefore deserve to keep it. While this myth implicitly condemns the many extremely wealthy who perform little or no philanthropy, it also celebrates a deeply anti-democratic process.

When extremely rich people make philanthropic "gifts," they decide individually what social causes to focus on, what problems to solve, and what activities to support. Their individual, private choices have social effects. We all must live with what a few extremely rich people decide to support financially. That is the opposite of democracy. If the people have to live with the decisions about how to spend large amounts of money, then the people should have democratic rights of participation in those decisions. That is the logic of elections, where all can equally cast their votes for the political leaders whose decisions all have to live with.

The US gives philanthropists tax reductions for the "gifts" they give away, yet that diminishes the funds available to the local, state, and federal governments. The government must, therefore, (1) cut the public services they perform, (2) raise taxes from others (often the nonrich), or (3) borrow to replace the revenue lost through rich people's "gifts." Service cuts or increasing government debt affect us all, yet a tiny minority of significant philanthropists' decisions impact our lives, even though that tiny minority is not accountable to us. Slowly, the government, and any form of democracy, lose control over wealth, while those thereby enriched have more and more influence to affect public life.

The cost of extreme wealth includes a major loss of democratic self-governance. We are long overdue a referendum on whether we as the majority support extreme wealth for a minority, given the damage that does to democracy.

The justification of obscene wealth based on its owners' social contributions is a carefully cultivated myth that equally carefully ignores all the considerations described above.

Capitalists deserve profits because they take risks

An old defense of capitalism: "Capitalists risk their money, energy, and time to start or expand businesses. Profit is their reward. Societies benefit from capitalists' risk-taking. Since profits are the incentive for capitalists to take socially beneficial risks, capitalists deserve profits."

No doubt employers take real risks. Enterprises can and do fail, losing capitalists' invested money and resources. However, capitalists seeking profits are hardly the only risk-takers.

In today's capitalist societies, all sorts of productions are undertaken without the involvement of profits. Communities build sports centers, children's playgrounds, and schools, for example, without profit accruing to those communities. Governments produce many different outputs without profit being the goal. Churches do likewise. All the above decision-makers take risks that their projects may not achieve their goals (which need not, and usually do not, include profit). Taking risks to produce goods or services neither requires profit nor justifies capitalism.

However, if the point of risk-taking myths is that risk-taking should be compensated, then one must ask: Why only compensate employers' risks? They are not enterprises' only risk-takers. In every enterprise, the employees, their families, and their residential communities also take risks.

Employees take risks when they go to work for a company. They become dependent on a job and income that could be lost. When choosing a job, employees and their families often devote their time, energy, and money to move into a community (with new schools for children to attend, new neighbors to befriend, and a new home to buy or rent). The risks that employees face depend on employer decisions over which the former have little or no power. Their employers may move production overseas or automate their jobs. Their employers may be unable (or unwilling) to pay taxes or repay loans and then decide to close the enterprise, depriving employees of jobs. Employees, their families, and their communities risk suffering the consequences of employers' profit-driven decisions about jobs.

Employees' incomes come from wages that pay for the labor power they sell to their employers. Employees are *not* paid for the risks they take. If employers demand and get profits for the risks they take, why does capitalism routinely deny employees shares of profits for the risks they take?

There is also an important difference between employees' and employers' risk-taking. The employers who take risks in starting or expanding an enterprise are also its key decision-makers. They know the details, conditions, and prospects of the risks they take. They have some ongoing control over the risks they take.

In stark contrast, the risks employees take depend on the employers' knowledge—from which employees are excluded. A good case could be made that the risks that employees face are, thus, actually greater than the owners'. Were profit really a reward for risk-taking, then profit should always be divided among all risk-takers. In capitalism, however, profits accrue not to workers but to employers. If employers are entitled to make the decisions about the businesses they risk starting and running, then workers too should share in owning and running the businesses because they take comparable risks by working there.

The notion that employers' profits are somehow justified by risk or risk-taking is a myth.

Profit Best Motivates Production; Capitalism Exalts Profits

Another myth holds that profit is the only (or most powerful) motive of production.

Profit is one among many motivators of people's actions. Love and hate, sex and jealousy, fear and greed, solidarity and loyalty are among the many others. Motivations can be material, as in cash, but they can also be symbolic, as in awards from well-reputed institutions.

Profit may motivate someone to provide a socially useful service. Profit may also motivate some socially regressive actions. Profit motivates drug and food companies to produce and sell dangerously adulterated products. Profits drive automobile producers to install devices that defeat pollution regulations. Profits sustain the cigarette, gun, pornography, gambling, and fossil fuel businesses, among many others whose social contributions are, at best, debatable.

On the other hand, Ludwig van Beethoven, Wolfgang Amadeus Mozart, Louis Pasteur, Albert Einstein, and countless other major contributors to modern life were not especially driven by any prospect of profits or obscene wealth. Most of them never obtained either.

The removal of profit from our economic system will not mean an absence of motivations, good or bad. Different economic systems use different combinations of motivators to secure different mixtures of behaviors. All struggle—using trial and error—to strengthen those motivators that inspire socially desired outcomes and to weaken those motivators that create socially unwelcome outcomes. All struggle with the motivators whose outcomes are mixtures of desirable and undesirable outcomes.

The myth of profit as "the great motivator" serves a purpose. In capitalism, employees labor to secure wages and salaries, not profits. Profits are the name of that portion of an enterprise's income that flows exclusively to its employers. Hyping profit as the sole or grand motivator serves to justify that flow to employers as if it were somehow good for society as a whole. Don't be fooled.

The notion that motivated behavior requires the capitalist system and its exaltation of profit is a myth.

Raising Wages Hurts Business and the Economy

This myth looks at only one side of a two-sided process.

Raising wages hurts business in one way and helps it in another. High wages raise the capitalist's costs of doing business, yet they also increase the purchasing power of the buying public. How each business fares in the balance between these opposing forces varies with each business's particular conditions. There is no one way that raising wages affects business in general, or an economy.

It is logical to suppose that some employers' profit rates are so small that raising wages (or any other of their costs) would lead them to close their enterprises. Yet logic likewise holds that raising some workers' wages will raise their incomes and enable them to spend more (including on the businesses whose wages rose). With more such spending, businesses may be able to sell more products, hire more employees, raise their prices, and so on. We cannot know in advance whether jobs lost exceed or fall short of jobs gained. Actual numbers of jobs lost or gained will, of course, depend not only on wage increases but on all the many other influences affecting employers' hiring decisions.

Why, then, are capitalists so often opposed to raising wages and to the efforts by employees and their unions to push for them? Part of the answer lies with employers' ignorance of economics and knee-jerk reaction to employees' demands for higher wages. If employers understood or acknowledged the contradictions of their system, they would avoid such reactions. Another part of the answer relates to what can happen if and when wages rise and some businesses (chiefly small and mid-sized) *do* collapse. Of course, that problem could be solved easily in a society that values and wants to preserve small businesses. A government subsidy and/or tax reduction could go to small businesses when they raise wages. That would help those businesses cope with rising wages while also helping the affected employees (useful since small businesses often pay lower wages than large businesses). A powerful movement of small businesses might ally with labor unions to push for such government support on the grounds that it helps reduce the social inequality between large and small business sectors.

A third part of the answer lies in the assumption of many employers that their expenditures on advertising will secure them the sale of all their products without needing to increase their employees' wages. Consumer debt will enable employees to buy the heavily advertised products without a wage increase. Believing that, employers will fight wage increases even when they grasp that higher wages will enhance employees' purchasing power.

In any case, the story of how raising wages is necessarily bad for business is a myth.

Capitalism Can Be Reformed

Throughout its history, capitalism provoked critics who (like myself) found it to be undemocratic, unequal, unstable, inefficient, immoral, and ultimately self-destructive. But others, the system's defenders, always insisted that capitalism was and is the highest level of economic and social development that humans can achieve. Among them, some admitted the system had flaws and weaknesses but believed these could be fixed by various adjustments that left its core unchanged. Those defenders of capitalism often came to be called *reformers*. Some of those reformers, disappointed in what reforms accomplished, came to believe that reforms were inadequate. The whole system, they concluded, needed to be changed from the ground up. They were often called *revolutionaries.*

Debates between reformers and revolutionaries are part of capitalism's history, just as they were also parts of the histories of other economic systems. For example, in the history of slavery in the US, there were those who approved and celebrated the slave system, but there were also its critics who wanted to reform slavery. Among reformers, some sought to get better food, clothing, and shelter for slaves. Some wanted to end the practice of breaking up slave families by selling their members to different buyers. Some focused on stopping or limiting various sorts of slave abuse by masters.

However, there were critics who rejected such reforms of slavery as fundamentally inadequate. They argued that slavery itself—the system in which some people owned and could thus buy and sell other people—was the problem to be solved. Making slavery less awful for slaves of African descent was not the issue, because such reforms, even if successful, were never secure. With continued slavery, whatever reforms masters had to accept could later be rejected by them. The continuation of slavery meant that, sooner or later, masters would have incentives to undo those reforms while the wealth they drew from their slaves gave them the power to do so. So long as slavery continued, the inequality and injustice of the relationship between master and slave persisted. Revolutionaries thus targeted the slave system itself. Rather than make it less awful for slaves, their goal was slavery's abolition.

In the history of capitalism, reformers and revolutionaries play parallel roles. Mentioned here are a few of many possible examples taken from US capitalism's history. After decades of difficult struggles, child labor in the US was eventually forbidden by law. Banking reform laws have typically passed after the more serious of many repeated banking system failures (including 1907, 1929, and 2008). Rules and regulations on railway safety usually followed the more serious accidents and derailments. Finally, the federal minimum wage (first legalized in 1938) aimed to reduce income inequality by placing a floor under wages.

Every one of these reforms was weakened or eliminated—often repeatedly—after it was enacted. As of mid-2023, the US Department of Labor was pursuing hundreds of ongoing cases of illegal child labor, with many more likely unreported as employers hired immigrants' children whose parents feared protesting to US authorities. After each of the many reforms of the US banking system, banks used their profits to evade, weaken, or end those reforms because they imposed profit-reducing constraints on bank activities. The 1999 repeal of the Glass-Steagall Act (a reform passed in 1933 responding to the Great Depression), led to the 2008–2009 bank-collapse catastrophe. After 2008–2009, we had further reforms, such as the Dodd-Frank Act. President Donald Trump rolled those back. Every few years, yet another banking system failure arises. Over the decades, many railway safety rules and regulations suffered similar profit-driven evasions, weakening, and repeals. Hence, the US has suffered innumerable railway problems, such as the February 2023 disaster in East Palestine, Ohio, that released hazardous materials into the nearby community. The US federal minimum wage was raised to $7.25 per hour in 2009. For the next fourteen years, it remained frozen at that level by the US Congress, even as consumer prices rose by over 20 percent.

Capitalism provokes reforms because of its profit-driven actions and their social consequences. In response, social movements arise demanding reforms. In turn, the reforms constrain profit maximization and thereby incentivize capitalists to fight against the reforms by blocking them, or at least delaying them (often for decades). Employers fight individual workers, labor unions, and social movements directly, but even more so via politics. They use their resources (accumulated profits, borrowed funds, etc.) to donate to parties and candidates, to hire and support armies of lobbyists working with elected officials, and to shape mass media coverage of their activities in fighting reforms. If mass action by social or labor movements still wins reformist laws, policies, and regulations, capitalists adjust their fight. Employers then focus more on evading, weakening, or repealing the laws and regulations. They use their profits to reduce or remove the constraints on their profits attributed to the reforms they object to. One way to do this became so commonplace that it acquired the name "regulatory capture": when government regulators are controlled by the employers they were supposed to regulate. Other ways include the relocation of enterprises to places where reforms do not exist or are not enforced, employment of immigrants whose legal status makes them fearful to report employers' violations of reformist laws and regulations, and various illegal activities.

The blocking and delays of reforms, like the subsequent evasion, weakening, and repeal of whatever reforms are achieved, damage the lives of millions of workers—and always have. There lies the basis for the revolutionary alternative. In a repetitive history, capitalism's organization of the economy—into employers and employees driven to profit via competition—provokes both reforms and opposition to those reforms. Few, if any, reforms are permanent; none are invulnerable to attacks by the employer class. The employers' ever-shifting profit opportunities determine how hard its attacks will target which reforms.

Beyond reform lies the possibility of system change. We could change the organization of workplaces to deprive any small minority from sitting atop and controlling the mass of working people. We could democratize enterprises such that all basic decisions (what, how, where to produce, and what to do with profits) are made by majority votes of all workplace participants. "One person, one vote" would be the basic principle governing the enterprise and the larger economy within which enterprises function. Multiple goals—not just profit maximization—would be what democratized enterprises strive to achieve. New problems and contradictions would animate such a post-capitalist economic system. Capitalism's intrinsic problems and contradictions—and the reforms they provoke—would fade into memories as people focused, rather, on doing better than capitalism.

Socialism Has Failed

After the 1989 collapses of Eastern European socialisms, capitalism's cheerleaders intensified their claims not just that those socialist societies had "failed" but that *all* socialisms—all its different forms—had failed. They treated those claims as if they were obvious, universal truths. However, there are multiple, different interpretations of the 1989 collapses, as there are of all important historical events.

While some regimes once widely identified as socialist have dissolved, especially in Eastern Europe, others have not, including the People's Republic of China, Cuba, North Korea, and Vietnam. Some forms of socialism have prospered quite dramatically, strengthening over the last thirty years. China's annual rates of GDP growth have been consistently about triple those of the US. China's growth rates for average real wages have exceeded those for US workers by even more. Vietnam's recovery from the extremely destructive US invasion and occupation has been remarkable and widely recognized as such. For over half a century, despite US sanctions and embargoes, Cuba has developed some of the most advanced educational and medical systems in the world. They now serve as models for many other countries.

The nineteenth century fostered the growth of socialism chiefly as a political and theoretical critique of capitalism. Socialists' practical experiments appeared in their formation of labor unions, anti-capitalist political parties, and anti-capitalist social movements. Socialists learned lessons along the way about which experiments should be preserved to become building blocks for a new post-capitalist system and which should be rejected as incompatible with that project.

The twentieth century saw one of these experiments, the taking of political power by Russian revolutionary socialists, confront the task of constructing a noncapitalist, specifically socialist economy and society. With the important exception of the localized Paris Commune in 1871, no post-capitalist construction of a nation or major region had been on the agenda of socialists before. The twentieth century saw Russia, China, and areas across the world erupt with socialist experiments in social and economic construction. All of these experiments in socialism (and others, such as Scandinavian socialism and social democracies elsewhere) have yielded a rich variety of lessons about (1) what was positive and should be preserved and (2) what was negative and should be excluded by twenty-first-century forms of socialism.

Capitalism did not spring fully formed from the ruins of feudalism, and socialism cannot do so from capitalism. Countless groups of early capitalists undertook experiments, and many did not last long, undone by feudal opposition, political mistakes, or lack of cultural acceptance. Early capitalist experiments were thus not simple "failures"; they generated crucial lessons for the eventual success of capitalism.

It took centuries for the necessary conditions to develop and allow later experiments in forms of capitalism to take off and become the model for modern global capitalism. In parallel fashion, nineteenth- and twentieth-century forms of socialism yielded lessons for twenty-first-century forms.

Over the last two centuries, socialism, as a combination of theories and practices of social change beyond capitalism, has become a powerful social movement across the world. Socialist theories and practices spread with and because of capitalism. Socialist newspapers, political parties, unions, political organizations, professional associations, and more became routine presences in most countries (including becoming governments in many). Socialists' demands often passed into law. Sometimes, the term "socialist" was explicitly involved. At other times, alternative terms ("social democracy," "democratic socialism," "the New Deal," "leftism," "radicalism," "eco-socialism," "socialist feminism," and so on) were used to describe parts of the broader socialist tradition. To condense all of that rich tradition of socialist theory and practice—much of it now sedimented into the laws, regulations, and customs of many nations—under the heading of "failure" makes little sense.

Within other social movements, such as anti-colonialism, disarmament, peace, anti-racism, feminism, and environmentalism, socialists repeatedly moved to effective leadership positions. Another great success of socialism has been the task of keeping alive—against massive repression and ideological warfare—the understanding that capitalism has systemic alternatives and that its profound problems might best be solved by changing to one of those alternatives.

Among socialism's failures has been the hesitance of so many of its adherents to go beyond focusing on the state in their work. Nineteenth-century European socialism focused strategically on capturing the state (via elections or revolutions) and then using state power to transition society beyond capitalism. Twentieth-century global socialism used that state-focused strategy to seize state power in many places. To this day, most socialists articulate their goals as having the state modify, lead, and regulate their economies toward greater wealth equality, less instability, and greater social justice. Most socialists still presume that the organization of production around employers (small groups of people that own and/or run enterprises) and employees (large groups of workers doing what employers tell them) is necessary or normal. Such socialists differ from supporters of capitalism because they believe the employers should be either private individuals subject to heavy state regulation and controls, or else officials of state-owned and operated productive enterprises.

Workers taking state power is, at best, a means; the end has always been a full social transition beyond capitalism. But, the socialist workers' states replaced private capitalists with state officials while leaving unchanged the internal organization of enterprises: the employer/employee structure inherited from capitalism. The overfocus on the state played no small role in enabling concentrations of power in socialist states that proved damaging to, and eventually destructive of, those socialist states. Many socialists came to criticize and reject those concentrations of state power. Yet most still do not articulate socialism's goals as including the end of the employer/employee organization inside workplaces and its replacement by a democratically run worker cooperative. Failure to do this has weakened a socialism that might otherwise have risen further given the deepening problems of so many capitalist systems today.

The history of twentieth-century socialist experiments attests to the trials, tribulations, and costs of transitions beyond capitalism that were begun and developed, but ultimately also blocked. It may not have been possible, under the actual conditions of the twentieth century, for socialists to go much beyond taking and stabilizing state power. However, there was no good excuse then—and there surely is none now—for not facing the contradictions, costs, and failures of being blocked from making the further transitions that had motivated socialists to seek state power in the first place. Refusing to face its experiments' contradictions and limits proved very costly to socialism. It is thus very important for socialists to do so now.

The declaration that "socialism failed" is as much a myth as the declaration that it is an achieved success. Socialism remains very much a work in progress.

Dismissals of socialism—as a "failure"—are sometimes undertaken with a different ideological purpose. Such dismissals refer to "the millions killed by Joseph Stalin and or Mao Zedong." The idea is to blame socialism and/or communism for what those particular leaders or regimes did. These are "count-the-deaths" sorts of historical arguments. Body counts are notoriously poor historical evidence, and all sorts of problems attach to blaming systems for what individuals do, but the argument surfaces often enough to invite a critical response. There is no question that the tumultuous transformations in Russia after 1917 and in China after 1949 were traumatic in many ways, and that a lot of people died. But that is also true of capitalism, only more so.

Shall we blame capitalism for the deaths caused by various leaders and regimes that presided over capitalist economies? How many tens of millions of deaths should be blamed, then, on the following: (1) European colonialism (for example, Britain's empire in India through Partition) during capitalism's ascendancy from the eighteenth century to the present, (2) World War I, fought by countries in which the capitalist economic system prevailed, and (3) World War II, likewise (including Russia's dead millions owing to Hitler's war against Russia)? Existing historical sources would suggest that deaths attributed to capitalist leaders, countries, and corporations outnumber those attributed to major Communist Party leaders like Stalin and Mao. Mass murder has been a part of the evolution of colonialism as the extension of capitalism. Dismissal of socialism on the basis of death counts reveals mostly the political biases and ideological goals of those who make such counts.

Chapter Five

The Relationships of Capitalism

The word "capitalism" has been used to refer to many different things. Were all writers to identify which particular meaning of the term each uses, no problem would arise. Sadly, that is not the case, and much confusion results from proceeding as if we all knew and agreed on some singular meaning of "capitalism." To avoid that confusion, this book tries carefully to acknowledge differences and explain *why* and *how* we understand capitalism in one particular way. Here, capitalism is that particular kind of economic system that organizes the production and distribution of goods and services in enterprises or workplaces divided between employers and employees.

This chapter of the book looks at how the capitalist economic system influences other aspects of modern societies. Capitalism is not the only cause of these other parts of society, nor are they always products of capitalism. However, prevailing ways of thinking largely ignore, or misunderstand, the relationships between capitalism and other important parts of society. For our purposes, such relationships highlight how capitalism contributes to so many social problems, and why solving those problems often requires challenging and moving beyond that system.

Capitalism and the State

The two most popular assumptions about the relationship between the state and capitalism seem nearly opposite. One side claims to see the state as a burden on the capitalist economy. The other side sees the flaws of capitalism as requiring government interventions into economic affairs to keep the system going. The anti-state side spends much time and energy demonizing the government and blaming state interventions in the economy for those shortcomings of capitalism they can admit. The more capitalism relies on government (favorable tax and tariff systems, subsidies, managing the money supply), the more urgently its anti-state defenders reject any dependency by capitalism on the state. History can help untangle these contradictions.

When capitalism became the dominant system in England and then spread to Europe, capitalism's celebrants wanted to emphasize their new system's break from feudalism. They adopted the French term *laissez-faire*—meaning a capitalism free from state interference—as a defining adjective of the capitalism they celebrated. For them, the forms of state they hated and rejected were the "absolute states" of late feudalism. That was the time of super-powerful kings and queens whose centralized power served to slow feudalism's decline. Those monarchs used their absolute state's power also to hobble emerging capitalists with constraints.

To break free from the monarchy's influence, capitalists forged alliances with all those dissatisfied with feudalism. They engaged in a revolutionary project that promised a new, republican system, with government democratically controlled by citizens, not kings. Runaway serfs who became capitalists' employees, merchants, growing industrial capitalists, independent artisans, and some other groups gathered in towns across Europe. From there, they challenged the feudal economic system, monarchism, and religious institutions allied with them. Capitalists celebrated their revolutionary movement as driven by the goals of liberty, equality, and fraternity. Capitalist employers joined serfs and their own employees in overthrowing old feudal governments, with the aim of thereby achieving transition from feudalism to capitalism.

Given their origins amid the absolute states of declining feudalism, revolutionary capitalists sought to overthrow feudalism to finally unchain their emerging capitalism. As the European transition to capitalism proceeded, beyond fights with a declining feudalism, a growing capitalism also provoked clashes between industrial capitalists and their employees. Capitalists realized that a strong state of their own could keep employees in line, producing surplus values for their employers. The state's police and military organizations could enforce laws protecting private property. A strong state could also mediate conflicts among capitalists. For example, when some capitalists took advantage of their market position to extract monopoly profits, other capitalists could utilize state power to regulate monopoly pricing. Capitalists needed strong governments, yet they also feared and resented them. That ambivalence never ceased.

Meanwhile, money itself—central and crucial for capitalism's development—proved badly vulnerable to corruption and instability in the hands of either governments or capitalist money lenders. Deals were struck to balance the power: monetary authority was vested in governmental institutions but required inputs from private bankers.

Again, capitalists recognized their dependence on government, yet they retained a deep inherited distrust of governments.

Capitalism's impetus for incessant growth also required military forces to protect existing colonies, access new colonies, and prevent capitalists in other countries from blocking that access. Colonialism and imperialism needed strong states wielding strong militaries. On the other hand, capitalists worried about the costs of such a military (how much they would be taxed for it) and the risks of putting too much power in government hands. What finally emerged from this tension is today's military-industrial complex, where capitalists profit from producing military goods and services sold to their governments. In return, the government shifts the huge resulting tax burdens (to pay for military goods and services) largely off capitalists and onto the working class.

The democracy that capitalists promised in their anti-feudal revolutions meant suffrage. However, restricted at first, that suffrage tended relentlessly toward universality. The problem for capitalists was always this: with truly universal suffrage, employers would never be more than a small minority of the voting population. Employees would be the majority. If employers and employees clashed within capitalism, universal suffrage would enable the employees to use the vote to overrule employers. The employees could undo the economy's unequal income distribution and reverse dominance from employers to employees. Rather than some monarch dictating to capitalists, it would then be employee voter majorities.

Capitalists "solved" the universal suffrage problem by developing systems to control elections and their results. They coupled universal suffrage with unequal influence based on buying votes, candidates, and parties, suppressing voters, and gerrymandering. All such mechanisms enable capitalists' money to control and shape voting.

Capitalists accumulate the wealth that enables them to do that; their employees do not.

Throughout capitalism's history, from its colonial past through its neocolonial present, it has had to navigate between its needs for and fear of a powerful state. The back-and-forth relation between capitalism and the state persists. To the extent that state action advances their interests, capitalists will support state power. To the extent that state power advances contrary interests of, say, employees, capitalists undermine, delay, distract, and denounce state power.

Capitalists have also evolved an ideal role for the state: to mobilize the general population to support capitalism, preferably with two or more political parties. That allows the staging of elections where one party, or coalition of parties, wins and rules until the next election, when it or another party/coalition wins and rules, and so on. What matters is that the different parties may disagree on a range of issues, so long as they all agree to maintain capitalism. For example, one party may appeal to and mobilize people who lean right while another party mobilizes people who lean left. Or one party may mobilize people who oppose abortion, celebrate guns, and embrace white supremacy, while another party supports abortion, wants to ban guns, and demands civil rights for nonwhite minorities. Whatever its platform, each party explicitly promises voters it will pursue its program and implicitly demands voters join in endorsing capitalism. Capitalists can fund two or more parties, confident in the knowledge that while policies on the explicit issues will vary with election outcomes, support for capitalism is assured no matter which party or coalition wins. In the US, the Republicans and Democrats perform the assigned roles. In many European countries, more than two parties do the same. There, even nominally "socialist" parties can and do participate in ways capitalists welcome and applaud. For good reason: all parties support and endorse the prevailing organization of workplaces in the capitalist manner of employers and employees. So long as this system secures capitalism in this way, capitalists can and do debate over the costs and benefits of strong versus weak government. And they need not care much about the debates' outcomes.

Libertarians are forever frustrated because they champion a minimal state as if it really mattered. They are ideological purists preaching to a choir of capitalists who mostly do not care. Liberals who want strong states to reform capitalism are also frustrated because the working class wants and needs reforms from capitalists who do not care. The capitalists tell both libertarians and liberals (including social democrats, etc.): "If you gather enough votes on the basis of endorsing and supporting capitalism, you can govern and tilt toward what you have promised your voters. Your tilt must remain 90 percent symbolic because it cannot compromise your basic commitment to endorse and support capitalism. If you do that," the capitalists explain, "we will crush and abandon you and bring a different party (or parties) to power." In fact, the capitalists rarely need to explain this to political party leaders and activists. In the words of Leonard Cohen's song, "everybody knows."

Capitalism and Fascism

Inside the workplace, capitalism relies largely on its own mechanisms to reproduce itself. Outside the workplace, it relies more ambivalently on market mechanisms and on the state's parliamentary and police mechanisms for self-reproduction. In so-called normal times, these mechanisms suffice. When these mechanisms are unable to manage the tensions and difficulties of capitalism, the system's reproduction is jeopardized. Fascism comprises a set of social changes made to enforce capitalism's reproduction when the "normal" mechanisms relied on for that reproduction fail. Fascism is a weapon in capitalism's arsenal for dealing with its most serious crises.

In fascism, the state's leaders and the top echelons of capitalists merge to enforce capitalism's methods of production. They often do this under the leadership and control of a fascist political party committed to arranging, sustaining, and controlling such a merger. Sometimes, various sorts of "external" threats provoke the turn to fascism. Sometimes, the "normal" cozy alliances between capitalists and state officials break down and thus "internally" threaten the system's reproduction. Then, the historical response to both external and internal threats has sometimes been transition to some form of fascism. Unified in fascism, capitalists and the government together try to destroy the groups challenging capitalism, such as labor unions, socialist parties, anti-capitalist intellectuals, and so on. Or, the merged leaders of fascism threaten actual or potential political adversaries into changing such that they become fascism's allies. In pursuing these objectives, fascism usually dispenses with the civil liberties and rights of capitalism's "normal times" by use of imprisonment, torture, and killing, likewise more than in "normal times." Hitler in Germany, Mussolini in Italy, and Franco in Spain offer many illustrations of these typical fascist methods. Economic and political power are centralized upward in the service of fascist power and capitalists' profit. That profit is then shared by capitalists and top state officials to reproduce capitalist relations of production, fascist organizations, and the governing alliance between them.

Frustrated by capitalism's instabilities, inequalities, and resulting social divisions, some employers and employees turn to the right, toward fascist political leaders who promise to "fix" capitalism's worst effects. Historically, fascist leaders have promised to secure full employment in a context of full social renewal that recovers a society's golden-age past of racial or ethnic purity (usually equated to racial or ethnic superiority). For example, Hitler sought to reestablish an Aryan German empire, the Third Reich; Mussolini, a renewed Italian empire; Franco, one for Spain. Using strong Keynesian-type monetary and fiscal policies and its quasi-state-capitalist merger, fascism can mobilize government policy and both public and private resources to achieve its goal of securing capitalist reproduction.

However, capitalism's cycles, inequalities, and deepening social divisions can also provoke a very different turn to the left: socialism. Socialists mobilize victims of capitalist cycles to ally with capitalism's critics. By means of organizations such as labor unions, socialist political parties, and allied social movements (among women, immigrants, and all sorts of persecuted groups), socialism became a global force across the last 150 years. While fascism uses concentrated wealth and political power to reproduce capitalism, socialism uses people power to challenge it. Both of these are responses to capitalist crises, but with very different goals.

Capitalism uses fascists and fascism to build a political counterweight against socialists and socialism. Socialist criticisms showed fascists that capitalism's flaws—especially instability and its social effects—had to be admitted. Solutions had also to be proposed. So, fascists crafted their analyses and solutions to strengthen and harden capitalism, rather than challenge it. Historically, fascist analyses blame outside agitators for capitalism's flaws, including selected foreign nations: Jews, Slavs, non-Aryans, and so on. Today's "culture wars" are part of this strategy too, blaming a society's problems on ethnic and religious groups, LGBTQ rights, women's rights, and so forth. Fascists often propose a social cleansing: a witch hunt to remove the "problems" from capitalism. Fascists work to destroy socialism and socialists. Again, Hitler, Mussolini, and Franco provide a long list of examples. Fascism envisions a "cleansed" capitalism that employs all, exalts the nation, and recovers its past greatness.

Fascism offers itself to capitalism as a mass base, counterbalancing socialism and its mass base. Where socialists battled capitalists and the state those capitalists dominated, fascists found friends and funders among capitalists and major allies among their politicians. Socialists and fascists confronted each other as parties during elections, but also in street battles and labor strikes. Capitalists clearly preferred the defensive alliance offered by the fascists over the socialists who, capitalists feared, favored a working-class newly empowered to dominate economically and politically. The closer socialists came to unionized power in capitalist workplaces and political power in the government; the more capitalists welcomed the fascists. The rising power of socialism across the nineteenth century motivated German, Italian, Spanish, and Japanese capitalists to accept fascist invitations. Other nations' capitalists were also tempted and flirted with their fascist leaders and parties.

Fascists learned that they had to play catch-up if they were going to win workers' loyalties away from the older and usually better-organized socialist movements. The Nazis did that, in part, by incorporating the word "socialism" into their official party name and actively soliciting workers to join the Nazi Party. Fascist leaders (for example, Mussolini) were sometimes veterans of socialist party leaderships who had quit to join the fascists. Capitalism provokes critics both left and right; it always has.

Capitalism produces fascism periodically: between the two world wars, it did so in Italy, Germany, Spain, and Japan. In those instances, economic and social traumas had shaken capitalist economies and societies out of their prior normalcy. The key example, Hitler's Germany, emerged from the distress of a fallen empire. After the Bismarck era had unified Germany, the country was a successfully growing empire. Yet, the accumulated shocks of losing World War I, losing the Kaiser (the German emperor), and suffering the reparations and hyperinflation that followed put the country into a state of general crisis. Germany's hyperinflation saw the exchange rate between US dollars and German marks rise from 160 marks per US dollar in 1922 to 4.2 trillion marks per US dollar by November 1923. In just a few short years, the savings and self-esteem of Germans shrank to nothing. When the Great Depression hit in 1929, it took Germany over the edge. An already-strained political center collapsed. German capitalists confronted the real possibility of a working-class blaming them and the capitalist system for their suffering. In 1932, the German left (both socialists – SPD - and the fast-growing communists – KPD) together accounted for half the nation's vote, and the Depression was still deepening. Catastrophe for capitalists loomed.

German capitalists felt they faced an existential threat. They were a very small proportion of the German electorate compared to the large numbers supporting socialists and communists. Because the only other comparable mass base that existed in Germany then were the Nazis, Germany's president invited Hitler to form a government. Hitler's fascism immediately and literally destroyed the socialist and communist parties—their social institutions, their legal status, and their leaders. Once in power, the Nazi Party effectively merged its top echelons with those of German capitalism to form an integrated, state-managed employer class. The fascist coalition at the top of German society kept capitalism safe from its socialist and communist challengers.

To secure their mass base, German fascists had to attract employees and self-employed people in significant numbers. To do that, they had to compete with the socialists and communists. Where socialists and communists focused their criticisms on the capitalist class and capitalism as a system, Hitler targeted Jews instead. Nazis constantly portrayed Jews as though all were rich and exploitative. In effect, Hitler substituted Jews for the capitalist class to poach on the socialists' and communists' strategies. It mattered little that most German capitalists were not Jewish and that most Jews were not capitalist employers. Scapegoating Jewish Germans served a major need of the capitalist class. It distracted the German working class from seeing capitalists and capitalism as their enemies.

Leveraging a mass base, a fascist leader like Hitler could negotiate an exchange: the Nazi Party's loyalties, votes, and support to German capital and capitalism, in return for capitalists' support for the Nazi Party and its government once in power. German fascism was the final result of that deal. Fascism got German capitalism through its crises (loss of World War I, hyperinflation in 1923, and the Great Depression in 1929) without changing the core organization of the capitalist system itself. Fascism got other capitalisms through their crises as well; it remains an option as crises afflict capitalisms.

Deepening inequality and a declining empire threaten crises for other capitalisms today: for example, in the US ever more people are questioning and criticizing the possibility of fascism. Recent elections and deepening social divisions have raised the question: Will US capi- talism move toward fascism too? We don't have fascism in the US yet. And if enough Americans understand this possibility and mobilize to prevent it, it may not arrive.

We face a crossroads in US history. Fascism means a population controlled by a government–capitalist merger intent on saving capitalism by enforcing its conditions. Socialism means a social system going beyond capitalism. These are unstable times in the economy, politics, and social fabric of our lives. Today, there are two big political questions: First, will an effective opposition to a fascist solution gather and prevail? And second, will an effective social movement for transition beyond capitalism arise and shape the nation's future?

Capitalism and Racism

In the US, as elsewhere, racism and capitalism struck a deal. Capitalism would perpetuate racism if racists responded by celebrating capitalism.

In earlier slave and feudal economic systems, small dominant minorities (masters and lords, respectively) accumulated disproportionate wealth and power vis-à-vis majorities (slaves and serfs). Some feudal and slave societies used racism to justify, manage, and maintain their class differences. They did this by designating some or all slaves or serfs as races apart from, different from, and inferior to the races of masters and lords. Like those other economic systems, capitalism adapted racism to meet its needs. Capitalists and their defenders crafted particular versions of racism to cope with several of their system's basic contradictions.

First among these is the division of the two basic classes of capitalism: employers and employees. What determined which individuals would rise to and stay in the dominating class? In a racist logic, if one race "naturally" had inherent characteristics suiting them to be employers (intelligence, command, discipline, etc.) while other races' characteristics suited them to be employees, then capitalism's class divisions could likewise be explained as "natural." With parallel logic, if one race were endowed exclusively with the skills and desires to wield social power over others, then society's class divisions simply followed as necessary for social order. In such logic, "nature" grades races as superior and inferior. Human beings cannot alter the natural order. For racists, it follows that it is ignorant folly—or worse—to try to do so.

When capitalism expanded, and competition among capitalists became global, capitalists reshaped the colonialism they inherited from earlier times to serve their needs. Not-yet-colonized territories were integrated into capitalist empires. Capital flowed in to produce raw materials and food for capitalists and workers in the colonizing countries. Sometimes, settlers communities dominated local economies; others used colonial administrations to shape local economic development. Old conceptions of race were adjusted, and forms of racism were developed to facilitate capitalist colonialism. Often using various physical traits (skin tone, body shape, etc.) to demarcate superior from inferior "races," the centers of capitalism then (especially European, but also North America and Japan) imposed racialized colonial subordinations on much of the rest of the world. Such racism helped to justify capitalist colonialism to the colonizers and to those among the colonized who became complicit with it.

Racist justification for colonialism existed long before Europeans brought African slaves to the Western Hemisphere. At first, European settlers there slaughtered and discriminated against Indigenous people, often using racist explanations for that behavior. That racism carried over to enslaved African people. Europeans separated themselves from enslaved Africans based on their distant homelands in Africa and their different cultures, languages, and skin tones. Europeans had had centuries to develop many kinds of racism to justify slavery, feudalism, and then capitalism.

However, racism in the US against African Americans has evolved its own particular mechanisms and forms across the generations of US capitalism. One form helps enable capitalism to cope with and survive its own instability. As mentioned above, US capitalism generally distributes the impacts of its recurring economic downturns unevenly. White populations lose less relative wealth and income than their fellow citizens of color. African Americans shoulder disproportionally more of the costs of and suffering from capitalism's instability.

White Americans can make and carry through life plans (to marry, raise a family, accumulate savings, build a community, develop skills, professional contacts, and credentials, etc.) with far-lower odds of having them disrupted by capitalism's instability. Unemployment imposed on white people occurs less often and lasts a shorter time, in general, than unemployment imposed on African Americans. White people get relative security from the ravages of the system's instability because it distributes those ravages unequally across the working class. Here lies one cause for white Americans' greater traditional sympathy for capitalism. To cultivate and strengthen that sympathy, capitalism uses (and thereby perpetuates) racism.

Put bluntly—as indeed it often is—the greater victimization of African Americans than white people within US capitalism is attributed to their racial identity. That sort of argument blames the differences between white and Black workers' economic participation and conditions on their different racial characteristics. It holds that Blacks are thus paid less, fired more often, and denied credit more often because their work is less valuable, their creditworthiness is poor, and so on. Racism is how many US capitalist employers have "managed" the system's unequal treatment of Black and white workers. Parallel racism has also been the way for many employees to understand the differences between white and Black workers' jobs and living conditions. And, throughout US capitalism's history, that "shared" racism has facilitated political alliances (as in the Republican Party over recent decades).

A slightly variant form of such racism arises in the form of opposition to redistributions of income or wealth. Such redistributions, according to this thinking, are not "deserved" or justified, because they would punish one race "who worked hard for it" while rewarding another race "who did not work hard for it." Parallel arguments discriminate against recent immigrants as lazy welfare-seekers, versus earlier (and usually white) immigrants who "worked hard." The ideological image here is a kind of meritocracy that rewards the harder workers. Racism congeals within such meritocratic delusions.

Social struggles to redistribute wealth have been tried repeatedly. They rarely work, and when they do, they rarely last. Were the root of wealth inequality addressed, struggles of redistribution could and would be avoided. Were incomes not unequally distributed in the first place—as capitalism does in its division of revenues between employees and employers—inequality would not haunt, disrupt, and destabilize the system as it always has.

Capitalism distributes wealth in particular ways that differ from those of alternative systems. Criticism of capitalism's wealth distribution ought to include a comparative examination of and debate over other systems' distributions. Capitalism's defenders fear where such debates might lead, so they tend to exclude system change from their discussion about capitalism's "distributional problems."

It remains too difficult for many Americans to see the huge injustice and the vast waste of human capabilities caused by racism against African-Americans, Indigenous people and immigrants. It remains too difficult for most Americans to imagine a different economic system, one that does *not* divide people into employers and employees and, therefore, neither needs nor allows racist justifications for the resulting inequalities.

In the minds of many, the mutual reinforcement of capitalism and racism is not conscious. Making their relationship conscious is an important component of the social movement to end both. In the US, overcoming racism requires confronting capitalism as one foundation of racism's reproduction. Overcoming racism requires a transition to a different economic system that refuses capitalism's defining division between employer and employee. In other countries, overcoming racism requires asking whether capitalism there plays a comparable role in reproducing racism of one sort or another. And, if it does, a similar program of transition will be in order.

Capitalism and the Environment

The demand upon every capitalist to grow is baked into capitalism. It's a kind of a carrot and stick. If you grow, you will gain an advantage over your competitors, but if you don't, they will gain an advantage over you. Capitalism pressures employers to function within a structure of rules that rewards increased profits and punishes reduced profits, so employers count only those costs that they are required to pay. Profit is what remains after an employer deducts costs from revenues. But all too often employers do not see, or refuse to see, the environmental costs. If a production process fouled the air, groundwater, soil, oceans, or animals; if it damaged the bodies and minds of workers; if it raised global temperatures—none of those environmental costs would need to be counted or paid by the employer. They are "external" to the capitalist system's world of costs capitalists have to pay (wages and material inputs).

Costs "external" for capitalists are *not* external for the larger society. For example, pollution from a factory's smoke exhaust might not be a cost for the factory's employer, but houses in the factory's vicinity would require more frequent coats of paint against the smog; people would need to visit doctors more frequently for respiratory diseases and make more visits to the laundromat to clean their dirty clothes. These are real costs paid by people other than the factories' capitalist employers.

These environmentally damaging, yet profitable projects often create social costs that exceed their private profits. Strictly speaking, if total (private plus social) costs exceed total (private) profits, efficiency requires that the project *not* be undertaken. But, since private capitalists count and consider only private costs and benefits in calculating their profits, they can and do undertake socially inefficient projects on a regular basis. Nothing better exposes capitalism's bogus claims to efficiency than taking environmental costs seriously.

In recent decades, political agitation by environmentalists has brought this situation to light. All kinds of public agencies have been established to identify and measure traditionally "external" costs, enabling new recognitions of costs never acknowledged before. Schemes have been debated over how to bring some of those costs inside the calculus of private capitalist investors (to convert "external" into "internal" costs). Governments now regularly require "environmental impact studies" before approving all sorts of infrastructure projects, or press investors to cover those costs as well as the usual "internal" costs. However, such steps are at an early age despite the fact that environmental degradation is at a dangerously advanced stage.

Recently, the concept of "green capitalism" has attracted public relations firms' interest. Industries often targeted by concerned environmentalists for their ecological misdeeds suggest that laws, regulations, and criticisms against those misdeeds are unnecessary. Capitalism will "solve," or already is "solving," our environmental problems. The system best solves its problems on its own, without government interventions. However, the logic here is highly debatable.

Capitalism created ecological damage because it was profitable. To leave the profit-driven system unregulated or unchanged risks that profits will continue to do what they did in the past: produce environmental damage that is difficult or impossible to reverse. When Russia's 2022 invasion of Ukraine and the associated sanctions drove up energy prices, prospective profits led to the temporary reopening of fossil fuel projects. In the past, responses to capitalism's other damages led to the attachment of adjectives such as "conscious," "socially responsible," "soulful," and "compassionate" to a hypothetically different capitalism. For a time (not long), the adjectives distracted attention from the noun. The adjective "green" will likely do the same for a while. Sooner or later, the underlying prioritization of profit for capitalists undermines all adjectives. The noun, "capitalism," and its imperatives prevail. Nothing better illustrates that point than today's green capitalism, forcing even our planetary survival to be subordinated to capitalist profiteering.

Capital still flows to where the profit rate is higher. To the extent that capitalists can evade the environmental costs of their investments, they will. So, too, will they promote "free market" ideology: that private profit calculations should alone govern investment decisions. In short, capitalism continues to fight for a private market efficiency that simply is not there. To protect their private market (and, more importantly, their profits), capitalists have spent heavily to persuade their employees to resist environmentalism and even fear it, threatening workers with job and income losses if employers ever have actually to cover environmental costs.

Capitalism, in its systemic pursuit of profit and growth, has been fundamentally destructive of our environment. The employer/employee relationship is the foundation of this system. More and more, the world is learning that we are approaching the point of jeopardizing humanity's survival. Having evolved through and changed from village economies to slave systems to feudalism and to capitalism, we know we can change our economic systems. We can do better than capitalism.

Chapter Six

Capitalism and You

We are all shaped by the people, institutions, and events surrounding our birth and growth. That means capitalism affects you in all the dimensions of your life. Not only does it shape our jobs, income, and working conditions; it influences our experiences of schools, friends, families, and literally everything else. The employer/employee system of production influences every relationship we have.

This book has discussed capitalism's undemocratic nature, general instability, inefficiency, the inequality it generates, the social problems it aggravates, and more. But now, let us explore how capitalism affects and shapes *you*, the reader of this book.

You Are Exploited

Right now, as you read this paragraph, you are being robbed. A chunk of everything your hard work creates is being taken from you. And it's capitalism that's robbing you. Every day, when you check in to work for your boss, you are being taken advantage of. You are being deprived of the full value of what you contribute. Let me break it down.

The pursuit of profits to accumulate money is simply *how capitalism works*. But where does this profit come from? That's where you come in. Profit comes from *you*. This process plays out across your city or town, your state, the country, and the entire world—the rich get richer, and most of the rest get by, even if only barely. We call the process—a boss's stealing from you— "exploitation." We don't mean that in an emotional sense. Exploited is not necessarily how we *feel* about it (though it could be). Exploitation is, in fact, a part of capitalist workplaces—the gap between how much value the worker produces and how much value workers get paid in wages or salaries. Exploitation is a universal feature of capitalist economies.

As described earlier in this book, everything about the work we do is designed to maximize the difference between what we get paid and the value of what our labor adds to what our employer sells. We all know it—maybe not consciously—but the name of the game is to rip us off, to forever try to make us produce more while paying us less. Employers put employees under a lot of pressure: "Work harder." "Work faster." "Spend less time in the bathroom." "Do not dawdle or distract your fellow workers or use the internet for amusement." In other words, do nothing that strays from the fundamental purpose of your job in the capitalist workplace: profit for employers.

Huge damages done to the physical, emotional, and mental health of employees follow. Work is where adults spend most of their lives. The workplace could support, enable, and encourage personal development, mutually enriching relationships, and learning from and teaching one another. Yet the human needs for all of those aspects of life, all of those means to happiness, are rarely served in capitalist workplaces. Depression, anxiety, despair, and hopelessness often follow. Likewise, employees usually lack the time, energy, and money needed to meet those needs outside the workplace.

The system requires capitalist firms to grow. That drives capitalists to exploit more: to pay workers less, make them work more, or make them more productive without increasing wages. When you see a corporation's CEO boasting about record profits, they mean your hard work is producing more value, but your wages are not hitting new highs. The capitalists take the value that the workers' labor creates and keep a large part of it for themselves. In effect, they steal it.

At most jobs, the condition of your employment is that you produce more by your labor than you get paid for doing it. So, in the capitalist system, the hard reality is this: no wage or salary earner is paid what they're worth. Capitalism means they get paid significantly less. All profit is value extraction: the worker produces it, and the employer takes it.

"Profit" is the name employers prefer for what they take from the value their workers' labor adds. Marx called what employers take the "surplus"—a word that focuses our attention on what the worker produces that someone else grabs.

Those who take the surplus from the workers hate to admit that. They prefer to see it differently. They, therefore, invented the term "profits" to mean a payment employers make to themselves for something crucial that they do. They "run the business." That is the equivalent of slave masters justifying the surplus they take from slaves' output as their payment for the work of "mastering." It is also the equivalent of feudal lords justifying rents imposed on their serfs as payments for the crucial task of "lording" over those serfs.

The revolutionary fact always was and is this: workers can do the work without masters, lords, or employers. In modern capitalist corporations, those who take the surplus—boards of directors—have literally nothing to do with the production of outputs. They mostly make big, long-term strategic decisions, give orders, and live luxuriously. A far-better system for workers would entail cooperatives of workers running their enterprises' production together, rotating tasks among themselves so all can understand and democratically run the business. This is examined further in the upcoming chapter, "What Comes After Capitalism."

Why So Many Hate Their Workplaces

At the end of every year, most corporations have a holiday party for all employees. At a certain point, the CEO (who is also a member of the board of directors) gets up on a wobbly table and thanks everyone. "You're all a great team," the CEO says, "and I want to thank each and every one of you for the contributions you made to another successful year here at the XYZ Corporation." In capitalism, the employees just thanked are totally excluded from any participation in deciding what happens to the fruits of their labor or to the profits generated by their labor.

Capitalism's rigid hierarchy characterizes nearly every workplace. An owner or board of directors sits at the top, giving orders to all ranked below them. Employees get no vote in choosing a business strategy for the enterprise in which they work and on which they depend. For most workers, once you set foot in the workplace, you are told where to stand, where to sit, when you can go to the bathroom, what to do, how to do it, and for how long. At day's end, whatever you helped to produce using your brains and your muscles *immediately belongs to your employers*. But they do sometimes give you a nice thank you at that party.

The US Census Bureau counts employers as 1 to 3 percent of the US population: a tiny percent of the whole. Employees, as capitalism's major other class, comprise, with their families, most of the rest. Employers typically accumulate wealth and power; employees typically do not. The resulting social divisions are the cages within which most people must pass their lives.

If that upsets you, if it eats at you over time, if it feels stressful and demeaning, it means you are a human being able to face your real situation. You understand why bar owners across America have window signs offering "happy hour." You grasp the signs' other message of consolation and understanding: the previous hours of the day at work were not happy.

That "happy hour" is part of a culture. You might call it the culture of capitalism, and here it is in a nutshell. The workplace is rarely where you seek, and even more rarely where you will find, personal fulfillment, recognition, enjoyment, relaxation, conviviality, friendship, or closeness. You might find those goals and joys of life in some corner of a workplace, maybe during a work break, maybe over lunch, maybe if you sneak around. But none of them are why you are there, nor are they what the employer wants out of or for you. Capitalism is disinterested in them. Capitalism exists to make profits for employers.

The "do what you love" Con

The emptiness, drain, and loss of self that happens in capitalist workplaces has been indirectly admitted even in mainstream neoclassical economics (the kind of economics taught in most schools and universities). Neoclassical economists mostly treat labor as intrinsically negative, a burden, a "disutility" workers suffer. They presume that labor is fundamentally unattractive: not a satisfaction, a gain, a relationship developed, or something learned. Wages are what make work tolerable for the laborer. Wages are the "plus" (or benefit), while labor is the "negative" (or cost). The job may be awful, but the wages enable you to go to the mall. Consumption is the compensation for work.

On that basis, many employers have used the slogan "Work doing what you love" to entice workers to accept lower wages, as if those low wages were necessary or reasonable since you get to do "what you love." Teachers, nurses, nannies, caring professionals, and others are told, "Your work is your reward." Employers also use workers' hopes for better jobs as a basis for paying them little for the work they actually perform. The term "intern" describes workers who get little or no pay from employers who promise to provide great letters of recommendation to potential future employers of such underpaid interns.

In still other ways, employers admit the awfulness of the workplaces they control and exploit. Some of them install fitness rooms, institute "casual Fridays," or organize occasional pizza parties. These are the in-house alternatives to "happy hours" at neighborhood bars. For employers, these are inexpensive outlays to offset job conditions that might otherwise cause workers to get sick, miss work days, leave for other jobs, or otherwise undermine employers' profits. No such additions to workplaces change the basic problem: profit-driven workplaces are mostly enemies of human relationships and growth. Our passions for what we love to do are neither enabled, nor encouraged, nor developed in or by capitalist workplaces. Rather, they are locations of many "unhappy hours" that workers suffer in capitalist systems, whether consciously or not.

The Ultimate Compensation for Labor Is Consumption

Beyond wages, capitalism's ultimate compensation for the burden of working is consumption. In capitalism, most people learn from an early age that work is your adult burden and consumption is its purpose. Consumption is to compensate for the frustration of your needs, desires, and creativity on the job. Feel bad on the job? Go shopping. Want to stop working for a while? Buy a vacation.

In this way, the capitalist gains twice. First, by exploitation, the capitalist appropriates the excess of the value added by workers' labor over the wage paid to those workers. Then, the employer can get us again if and when they charge us more for goods than it really costs to buy the employer's output. Then employers get you twice—as a worker and as a consumer.

Workers, as they fall ever further behind employers in terms of wealth, income, power, and culture, may accept this reality if they attain an ever-rising level of personal consumption. Your exploitation is easier to tolerate, or even forget, when you can afford to go to the movies, buy a new car, or go to college. Generations of capitalism's champions have firmly believed that a secure capitalism is one that delivers a rising standard of consumption to its working classes, because if it doesn't, workers will notice and challenge the system. For capitalism to succeed (or even survive), two goals must be achieved: (1) real wages must rise, and (2) workers must believe that rising consumption is an adequate, appropriate reward for their work.

This is where consumer ("household") debt comes in. Over the last forty years, US workers' wages have barely risen above the rate of inflation. To keep up with the American dream that was relentlessly advertised to them, workers had to find rising purchasing power elsewhere since their real wages were stagnant. The solution was borrowing via credit cards, car loans, and mortgages (later supplemented by student loans). In effect, what employers saved by not raising real wages (as they had before 1980) they then lent to those same workers. Employers thus funded the borrowing workers undertook *because* employers stopped raising real wages. Employers benefited by constraining real wages, and thus boosting profits, plus earning interest payments on workers' rising indebtedness.

The US capitalist system generated record profits over most of the last forty years. Yet it also left a trail of costs in its wake: rising debt, rising debt anxiety, and widening income inequality.

Unemployment: Capitalism's Cruel Absurdity

Unemployment—being jobless when you do not want to be—follows capitalism's cyclical downturns every four to seven years on average. When unemployment rises, so do depressive disorders, alcoholism, drug abuse, marital problems, child abuse, and criminal behaviors. What goes down with rising unemployment includes individual workers' self-esteem, personal savings, and physical and mental health. This list barely captures the billions in lost or wasted value and the massive human suffering caused by capitalism's recurring unemployment.

It is a profound and enduring inefficiency of capitalism that every four to seven years, it throws millions of people out of work, often for years.

Employers too suffer from unemployment. Employers know, even if they don't admit it, that the only way they profit is if their employees are working. Without the employees, factories, offices, and stores produce no profits.

Yet unemployment has persisted across capitalism's history despite its wasteful, cruel absurdity. A proper, well-functioning economy would connect unemployed people who want and can perform work with idle tools, equipment, and raw materials to create socially useful products. After all, since the unemployed continue to consume, common sense suggests enabling them to work. However, capitalism reproduces unemployment for one profitable reason: it scares and thus "disciplines" workers.

Periodic bouts of unemployment teach the working class a basic lesson: however poor the job, it is better than unemployment. When unemployment shoots up, workers worry, "Will it hit me too?" Such worry is often as bad as unemployment itself, and it motivates workers to accept otherwise-inadequate conditions and compensation. Unionized workers have often accepted contracts with lower wages if they include job-security commitments. Employers regularly threaten workers, individually and collectively, with dismissal to wring concessions from them.

A major reason for so many bad jobs being accepted is that they are better than unemployment. No wonder unemployment is allowed to return so often; it serves a purpose in and for capitalism.

Capitalism and the Individual: Which Shapes Which?

The extremely conservative economist Milton Friedman celebrated a private capitalist system. He wanted the government to play the most minimal role possible in terms of intervening in the economy. Private capitalist enterprises should manage economic activities (production, distribution, etc.) and be protected from the government. Nor should they be vulnerable to popular expectations about their behavior. A capitalist's job, he said, was to make money, to profit from that capitalist's business. Interpreting Adam Smith, Friedman insisted that if each and every employer and employee pursue their own personal gain (wage/salary for the employee, profit for the employer), the end result would be the best-possible economy and society for all of us.

In other words, if I ignore the impact of my actions on everybody else, if I ignore my community's needs and instead pursue my own personal gain, it will all work out for the best for everyone. Is this, as Friedman thought, the key to social well-being? Or is it a crude and quite imaginary justification for total selfishness?

Where do our morals and ethics come from? For Friedman they are innate: persons are born good or not, with original virtue or original sin. Alternatively, are we shaped by the social institutions—the families, schools, workplaces, communities, religions—into which we are born and with which we live, grow, and change? Might those institutions help shape our moral values, sense of self, and relationships with others?

We need not choose—as Friedman did—one or the other: that individuals shape society *or* that society shapes individuals. Both can be true: individuals, profoundly shaped by their social and natural environments, also react back upon and shape those environments. The world may well be a place of endless interactions, both among individuals and between them and society. The interactions change both sides; that in turn changes their interactions, producing that endless process we call history.

Anyone who puts forward capital—money—to hire workers, and set them in motion with raw materials, tools, and equipment to secure a profit is thereby defined as a capitalist. It is their actions that define them as such. They occupy a position (employer) within the capitalist system of production. The goal of that position—as dictated by how the system works—becomes the goal of persons who wish to occupy the employer position. Employers may say that their goals are lofty social ideals of all sorts. However, down in the "real world," where the capitalist system is the established mode of producing and distributing goods and services, capitalists have one dominant, ultimate, bottom-line goal: profit. Profit maximization gives each capitalist the best-possible chance of staying in the position of employer, rather than sliding down into the employee position, or worse.

Capitalists need not be personally greedy, though some surely are. Nor are they necessarily "bad" or "good" as people, as individuals. However, in their position as capitalists/employers, they need to act in certain ways or lose that position. The system dictates profit maximization as the employer's best shot at keeping their position. The system sets capitalists in competition with one another; the activity of each threatens the others. As the laws of the jungle drive animals to struggle and literally eat one another, so do the laws of capitalist competition drive ruthless, aggressive behavior of one capitalist against the others. And, of course, the laws of the capitalist system shape the individual employers and employees, much as the laws of the jungle shape the animals living in it.

Individualism gone wrong

At its birth, capitalism's enthusiasts claimed the system institutionalized the individual freedom to aspire and achieve without interference or constraint from government or church. Through capitalism, individuals could break out of the rigid social roles the previous society had imposed on the vast majority of people (slaves and masters, serfs and lords). Capitalism would enable each individual's skills, ambitions, and energies to bring them positions in society never before possible for the masses of people. Previous societies and their representatives, especially strong states, were the enemies. Capitalism would vanquish them and liberate individuals from their rule. "Individualism" was capitalism's banner (which is one reason "socialism" became its great adversary).

Over the last two centuries, individualism grew into a major philosophy of capitalism. It led many to disregard how societies shape the individuals raised within them. Many forms of individualism thus stipulate that individuals have certain "innate qualities" that create and shape society. The close association of capitalism and individualism, unsurprisingly, provoked capitalism's critics to take the name "socialism." Such critics tend to emphasize how society shapes individuals.

Capitalism has often compromised the individualist promises made at its beginnings. Consider our society's deep psychic wound of loneliness. Capitalism breeds many individuals who feel unjustly, bitterly cut off from any community. Trained to think that their individual characteristics determine their social positions, employees often blame their positions in capitalist society upon themselves, upon their individual qualities. Consequent brooding undermines interpersonal communication and trust. Overcoming such tendencies sufficiently to combine with others in voluntary collective action, even when democratically organized, becomes very difficult and thus rare. On the other side, employers indulge the individualist view that they "made themselves." Denying their own socialization, they slide into feelings of innate superiority based on what employers often think are their "inherent" qualities and the lack of them among employees.

Feelings, sensibilities, and aspirations are shaped by all the encounters in our lives. The particularities of the capitalist economic system—and especially its core structural division between employers and employees—influence many of those encounters. Among the effects of capitalism and individualism are the widespread loneliness people feel, the weakness and fragility of their connections with others.

Even Plato and Aristotle, thousands of years ago, addressed a parallel undermining of community when they criticized markets. They believed that markets undermined what they called "social cohesion," what we might term "community" or "solidarity." Their criticisms apply to capitalism as well since it expanded and celebrated markets far beyond what earlier systems had done. Critics of markets have long argued that they lead participants to ask, "How little can I give up, for how much can I get in return?" In market exchanges, others become instruments for our gain. Market relationships are transactional, adversarial, and self-serving. They weaken social solidarity and produce a deeply lonely population.

Capitalism by now has generated an extreme individualism that divides us. As children mature, they are told that the pursuit of personal profit is natural. We are given rags-to-riches stories to strengthen our motivation to pursue wealth no matter what happens to others. We are warned about trusting others, about their ulterior motives, and their gains from cheating us. Individualist ideological blinders prevent many from asking how the system into which we were born might be a key problem and system change might be a key solution.

The ironic contradiction of individualism is that it leads to loss of respect for many individuals. Individualism often discredits the individual who does not live up to impossible expectations. It then deprives individuals of both their own self-support and that of family, friends, and coworkers around them. Individuals who do not realize capitalism's role in their lives often suffer loneliness instead of collaborating with others to go beyond capitalism and its destructive individualism.

Capitalism trains you to accept the suffering of others

This unchecked individualism also trains people to accept and justify the horrific consequences of capitalism, because those are blamed on its victims.

Capitalism, Marx theorized, displays "uneven development." While it generates great wealth, it also generates great poverty. For every part of a major capitalist city that is rich, another is poor. In the US, the dynamic center of capitalist growth was first New England, then the industrial Midwest, then the Southwest, in a pattern of uneven development that saw each of those regions fall after they had grown. In the US and elsewhere, endless "anti-poverty policies" and "wars on poverty" have failed to end it.

In the 1970s, Detroit was a center of US capitalism, with a population of nearly two million. It paid workers better than in most parts of the US; those workers had strong unions. It was the global center of the automobile industry, a vital part of capitalism. Today, Detroit has been "undeveloped" by capitalism. Its population has declined to less than seven hundred thousand, and vast sections of the city are impoverished or abandoned.

Capitalism's profit drive shifted investible funds from Detroit to other locations where automobile production was more profitable. That happened partly because those locations lacked Detroit's strong union and anti-capitalist movements among autoworkers and those movements' allies. Yet alternative narratives—that Detroit's demise was somehow its own fault—survive and, in many areas, prevail. Individualist accounts blame the victims: the workers did not work hard; business owners didn't innovate enough; wages or wage demands were too high; local politicians were corrupt. For the last forty years, as Detroit descended into a permanent crisis, very little was done to stop and reverse the decline. Few criticized capitalism and its profit-driven, uneven development as a main cause of Detroit's demise (an early exception was Marvin Surkin and Dan Georgakas, *Detroit: I Do Mind Dying; A Study in Urban Revolution*, 3rd ed., Chicago: Haymarket Books, 2012 [1975].

The same applies to countries. The dynamic "center" of capitalism also developed unevenly as it moved from England (seventeenth and eighteenth centuries) to western Europe to north America and Japan. More recently it has moved on to China, India, and Brazil. Regions built up by capitalism's movement coexist with regions declining because capital accumulation, and thus capitalist development, have moved on.

In capitalism's long commitment to colonialism, each capitalist "center" developed on the basis of wealth stolen from the colonized "periphery" and labor exploited there (or as immigrants inside the colonizer country). Capitalism relied on labor and resources drawn from across the globe, but it concentrated the resulting wealth in a few colonial centers. Uneven development is built into capitalism's structure. Capitalism's neocolonial phase continues uneven development into our era.

Capitalism conditions many to believe that in nature or in the economy, when something goes up, something else must go down. People who might otherwise celebrate and welcome an end to poverty resist doing so by means of changing the economic system. That resistance is informed partly by an individualism that blames poverty on the poor. Anti-poverty programs thus often focus on changing the poor individuals, rather than changing the system that impoverishes them. That resistance is also partly fueled by the belief that helping the poor out of poverty will necessarily press others down into poverty. One part of the working class fears that help for another part will come at the first part's expense. White workers fear assistance to Black workers will come at white workers' expense. Since employers gain from such beliefs, they often repeat and exaggerate them.

Recently, right-wing politicians often mobilize people against immigrants around the world, using the argument that aiding them would necessarily cost nonimmigrant workers. All around the world there are anxieties born of capitalism and the inequalities it perpetuates: if I have something, helping others will be at my expense.

Such fears shape how we interact with others, and what we consider acceptable treatment of other people. Causes of those fears include capitalism. Its uneven development shapes those fears.

Ignoring how capitalism works—how capitalists (the few) take surpluses produced by others (the many)—serves to exonerate capitalism's responsibility for its negative social effects. By their taboo on blaming capitalism, the system's defenders foster the blaming of those effects on something or someone else. Thus the poverty and misery of the global South is more easily tolerated if seen as the effect of "other" cultures, inadequate work ethics, or corrupt politicians. By doing nothing about the capitalist system, uneven development continues in all its forms (unequal income and wealth distributions, cyclical instability, politics corrupted by wealth, etc.).

Provoked to protest these horrors, individuals learn, eventually, to understand them as social problems rooted in specific economic systems. That understanding enables the social movements that chal-lenge capitalism as a key cause of those horrors. Challenges evolve into finding solutions that overcome capitalism's "uneven development" by replacing capitalism itself with a different economic system.

Living in the Contradictions of Capitalism

We live in a capitalist system, with all the contradictions and flaws discussed in this book. We therefore accommodate capitalism in a thousand ways, consciously and unconsciously, as life in any system requires. Yet we can also seek, form, and share a critical understanding of capitalism. Doing so offsets our necessary accommodation with movement toward social change beyond capitalism.

If I could give this book's readers any advice, it would be to talk about the real contradictions with which we live. Understand and recognize the accommodations you've made to capitalism and why you have done so. Admitting them and their costs to you and others can lead directly to hoping for and believing in the possibility of a better system, a better way to live. We can do better than capitalism, just as people like us long ago insisted that they could do better than slavery, feudalism, monarchy, and so on. But it will take time, energy, and resources to move society in that direction.

The word "utopia" defines certain dreams and imaginary futures that people have always experienced or felt: of better conditions, better relationships, better lives. It is important for one's mental health to have utopian fantasies, even as you also recognize the distance and tension between the life you actually live and the utopia you dream of. Such recognition can bring that utopia closer. Utopian visions were always important parts of social movements to change economic systems in the past. They are important in the same way now.

Criticism of capitalism is not nihilism, not a simple rejection of what is. Understanding capitalism critically has mostly been accompanied by the dream, the movement, the gesture, the hope, the belief: we can do better. People made it better in the past and can again. Employees are capitalist society's masses, like slaves and serfs in slavery and feudalism. All those masses have been trapped within systems. All have sought escape or revolution, and eventually achieved them. And you?

From the basics of the capitalist class structure—organizing workplaces into a minority that controls and exploits a majority—to all its influences upon the economy, politics, and culture, a conclusion emerges. Capitalism shapes us all in countless ways. If the current social system offers a life with many problems, instabilities, and injustices, then an honest logic leads us to question and even challenge the role of capitalism in causing and sustaining the difficult conditions of our lives.

Capitalism is not the only cause of the conditions of our lives; no one thing ever is. But capitalism cannot be excluded from among the causes, and it cannot be excused from blame, as so many try so hard to do. This book reestablishes capitalism's role in the issues we face today. That is urgently necessary now, after Cold War decades of a near-absolute taboo on criticizing capitalism coupled with deeply instilled fears of demonized alternatives. If we grasp our suffering's relationship to capitalism and understand capitalism critically, we have the ability to decide that system change is one key step on the road to doing better in the future.

Chapter Seven

What Comes after Capitalism

Economic system changes *have happened before*. All past economic systems were born, evolved over time, and then passed away as other systems emerged to replace them. All past societies have had people who thought about changing their lives for the better, and who came to understand their society and its economic system (or systems) critically. Those people then got together in social movements aimed at transitioning from the system they had to one they thought could work better. There were always people whose attitude toward the existing system was, "This is the best we can do." There were always others who said, "This needs to change." This difference and division agitates today's capitalism, too.

Capitalism is always changing, but for long periods, the basic system has retained certain features. Those consistent features make up what we mean by "the capitalist system"; they are how capitalism is defined in this book. The central feature is the organization of workplace participants into a small minority exploiting and directing a large majority. Across an infinity of changes in capitalism, the basic contours of employer versus employee have endured.

That employer-versus-employee structure is a key, core problem of capitalism. To go beyond capitalism, then, means going beyond that structure. It means rethinking and reorganizing our workplaces, our factories, offices, stores, farms, households, and so on. What can emerge out of capitalism's decline are new, differently organized workplaces. We can accomplish that reorganization as the basis for a different, better society and different, better lives for all of us.

Imagining a Better Way

To discuss where society might go is risky. No one knows the future. History is always open ended. Looking back, it seems clear that system changes occurred when and mostly because existing systems were no longer tolerable. At those times, there was relatively little clarity or agreement as to what the next system would entail, beyond a few vague basics. But that did not stop system changes from occurring.

Slaves who found slavery intolerable sought "freedom." Serfs sought "liberty." Many others added "equality," "fraternity," and "democracy." It wasn't clear what such terms meant concretely until, by trial and error—and luck—a new system congealed in place of the old one. Slaves could not predict the post-slavery future, nor could serfs predict the post-feudal future. Today, employees cannot precisely predict the post-capitalist future. Yet, once again, the demand for change in an intolerable present system is making social change happen.

However, there are always some whose particular ideas influence the construction of the next system. Moving beyond capitalism is no exception. A good part of this book uses the work of Marx and Marxists because their tradition pioneered and accumulated system-focused criticism of capitalism and also practical experiments in constructing post-capitalist systems.

Many of the Marxist experiments to construct post-capitalist systems over the last century were complex, mixing different elements despite almost always choosing the name "socialism" for what they did. The mixtures included positive achievements on which to build and big mistakes to avoid repeating. The defining feature of most socialist experiments was a focus on the state as a regulator of, or replacement for, private capitalists. While those attempts made progress in defining what collective consumption is and how it might be organized, they failed to move much beyond the capitalist organization of workplaces into employers and employees.

From the moderate socialisms of Scandinavia and Western Europe (with the state as regulator of private enterprises) to the Soviet Union–type socialisms (with the state as owner/operator of enterprises) and all the hybrid socialisms in between (e.g., the People's Republic of China), one basic reality stands out: the basic capitalist organization/structure of employer versus employee remained across them all, even as the precise nature of who occupies the minority position of employer often changed. Private individuals as employers changed to state officials (individuals occupying positions within a state apparatus) as employers. In short, largely private capitalism changed into state capitalism or hybrid combinations of both kinds. The "who" changed, but the structured positions of employer and employee did not. Were these socialist experiments in going beyond capitalism flawed or incomplete <u>because</u> of the survival of the capitalist structure within them? This book answers <u>yes</u>.

What, then, is to be done?

The Case for Worker Cooperatives

Cooperatives (and specifically worker cooperatives) are a critical component of building a more sustainable, equitable, and democratic future. Worker co-ops represent a crucial next step in doing better than capitalism—a real alternative to it.

A co-op is a business or workplace that is directed and operated by all its members on the principle of "one person, one vote." There is no employer (owner, board of directors, or CEO) making basic decisions (what, how, and where to produce, and what to do with the surplus or profits) while excluding the employees. Worker co-ops operate through democratic control by all their members. Members' values and goals govern. They decide democratically what priorities will determine their basic decisions about their workplace. Typical priorities include making workplaces into egalitarian, sustainable, and joyful communities where human relationships and individuals' personal development and growth can flourish. Worker coops' priorities may include profit maximization, but always as only one among many other equally or more important goals.

The management structures and day-to-day operations of co-ops can vary greatly according to the needs and desires of the co-op members. Co-ops exist in many varieties, including worker, consumer, producer, sales, purchasing, and multi-stakeholder configurations, among others. Each of these structures matches people's particular needs to a particular collaborative approach.

In a worker-co-op-based economic system, the employer/employee difference disappears. It no longer organizes workplaces such as factories, offices, farms, and stores. Instead, for each participant in a workplace, going to work becomes functioning within a democratic community.

In that community, carefully prepared information relevant to basic workplace decisions is distributed to all well in advance. Workers are paid to study that information; it is part of their work, their job description. All workers' inputs are welcomed, all options openly debated and voted on. In terms of Marx's notion of the surplus generated by productive workers, in worker co-ops it is those workers themselves who appropriate and distribute the surplus generated in the workplace. No separate class of employers does that. Thus, a democratic worker co-op represents a step outside and beyond capitalism's employer/employee structure. Worker co-ops overcome capitalism's class divide. The workers control the full fruits of their labor.

Worker co-ops already exist in modern societies (as they also did throughout much of history). Today, they coexist alongside capitalist enterprises. In modern capitalism, they form the embryonic beginnings of a possible future economic system. They played parallel roles in pre-capitalist economic systems, too. As those systems declined, worker co-ops might have been the next system that emerged from a prior system's decline. However, in reality, other, different systems emerged (in Europe, feudalism out of slavery's decline, and capitalism out of feudalism's decline). There is no necessary sequence of change. Capitalism's decline opens the space for the next system to emerge. Whether that will be a worker-co-op-based system or not depends on the people making the transition. Where do such agents of transition wish to go in terms of organizing their economy? If workplace democratization is high on their agenda, the hierarchical divisions of slavery, feudalism, and capitalism will be what they avoid. Worker co-ops may well, then, be where they take societies in transition.

Worker co-ops offer democracy

As residents of our city, state, and nation, we have at least a vote for the mayor, governor, or president; but in capitalist factories, stores, and offices, comparable voting is not allowed. There, the CEO often functions like a king.

Worker co-ops end such mini-monarchies inside capitalist corporations. If societies have a commitment to democracy, then democracy surely belongs first and foremost where most adults spend most of their adult life—at work. Yet in the US and most other capitalist nations, from their beginnings, democracy was always excluded from most workplaces. No wonder CEOs' speeches praising democracy ring so hollow.

Democratic workplaces are just the beginning. Co-ops can be schools of democracy, training masses of people in how to use, protect, and improve democratic procedures and values. Workers trained in democracy at work can inspire and train others to install democratic decision-making in all other areas of society. In today's so-called democratic nations, democracy merely means annual mass voting for political authorities. Even if corporations and the rich did not manipulate such elections (as they do now), real democracy requires much more than such elections. Democratic workplaces give people a daily experience with democracy. That will develop the appetite to have a comparably real democracy in politics as well: everyday, ongoing democratic inputs, not merely annual elections.

Truly democratic societies require democratized workplaces. They always did.

Co-ops are driven by more than profit

In a worker co-op, the enterprise has multiple goals. While it seeks revenue greater than costs, its members also want job security, safe work environments, socially meaningful work, and jobs that encourage and support friendships and individual workers' learning and growth. Together with other stakeholders (for example, the residential communities surrounding workplaces), worker co-op members consider their profits, their wages, the social and natural environments they live in, and their personal and collective development all together. It is an institutionalized way of having more objectives than profit and making decisions democratically, with all stakeholders and their diverse workplace objectives included.

Removing profit as *the* single motive of an enterprise can also encourage innovation differently, even more so, than capitalism usually does. Capitalist businesses will cut their labor costs, change job descriptions, and fire employees whenever it serves their profitability. They will likewise change the products they market, the technologies they deploy, the locations they choose, and the advertising they buy to maximize profitability.

In capitalism, if a new technology automates the employee's work, making production more efficient and the enterprise more profitable, employees have good reasons to worry about their job security and to oppose the new, efficient technology. Worker co-ops could respond differently to technical change. Instead of replacing workers, a better machine might replace half of the workers' worktime. Technology would then enhance workers' leisure rather than employers' profits. Which is better for the long run of each enterprise is an open question. Are the workers exhausted, and therefore in need of more time for friends, family, and leisure? Which is better for society: more profits for the employer minority or more leisure for the employee majority?

What could the co-op do with more profits? Worker co-ops, which serve the needs and desires of their majority through democratic process, would be far less excited, or able, to fire their companions for a profit. Worker co-ops would be far more sensitive to many of those social and environmental costs of production, and far more likely to include them in the calculations informing their business decisions.

Worker-owners have a commitment and loyalty toward their cooperative workplace rarely found among employees constantly told by "higher-ups" what to do at work. Why should we be surprised when employees care less about a business that exploits them and treats them like a disposable tool for profit? Workers who direct their own co-op businesses are engaged in democracy for which they feel responsible and loyal. Worker co-op members are more likely to go that extra step that capitalist employees do not. No wonder research (such as that by Professor Virginie Pérotin of Leeds University in the UK) on comparable businesses that differ only by their structures—capitalist versus worker co-op—shows the latter to be more efficient and last longer.

Co-ops are a force of equality

With direct democracy and a structure that elevates priorities such as saving the planet, the quality of human life, and work–life balance, cooperatives can be a driving force for equality. In 2014, a survey revealed that the average US worker believed the typical CEO-to-worker pay ratio in the US is 30:1. The reality was much starker: CEOs got paid $354 for every $1 a typical employee makes. The workers of Amazon and Tesla would never vote to approve paying Jeff Bezos or Elon Musk what they receive today from these companies. Workers would never vote to pay themselves an hourly wage so low that they must get second and third jobs, while top managers and major shareholders take enough to buy megayachts. The same people who guessed the CEO-to-worker pay ratio was 30:1 said their desired ratio would be 4.6:1. The inequalities of our current system would not survive votes by democratic majorities of worker-co-op enterprises.

Notions that hierarchical, top-down power and decision-making are necessary or natural will disappear from the economy just like the old notions that society needed a king who worked directly with God. Working people will come to understand themselves no longer as akin to slaves, serfs, or employees. Rather, they will self-identify as equally important members of their residential communities and likewise their workplace communities. In worker co-ops, they will exercise their democratic capabilities by designing and deciding the enterprise's future alongside others as parts of everyone's job descriptions.

Of course, cooperatives have and will face growing pains in this process. Equality will not be perfect or instantaneous simply due to a switch to cooperativism. But, just as capitalism was an evolving improvement from feudalism, cooperatives will evolve as well.

Transitions Are Normal and Take Time. We're Not Done Evolving

The transition from capitalism to a worker-co-op-based economic system is already underway. Over a long time and in many places, powerful social forces brought worker co-ops into existence. The flaws and difficulties of slavery, feudalism, and capitalism *pushed* workers to imagine workplace alternatives, including democratic co-ops.

Yet transitions are overdetermined by everything happening in their economic, political, and cultural environments. As such, they are filled with contradictions and change unevenly. Transitions happen here but not there. Sometimes the transitions are quick; at other times they drag and delay. Some democratic enterprises might not understand themselves as transitioning systems, while others focus on it.

Cooperatives of all kinds have long, complex histories. In many parts of the world today, they have carved out acceptable places, often on condition of remaining relatively small, within otherwise-capitalist economies. Worker co-ops, and those who advocate for them, rarely confront capitalism explicitly, as the representation of an alternative economic system. They likely fear capitalism's probable reaction. Nonetheless, this confrontation could take many forms.

More labor unions could add the establishment of worker co-ops to their strategies when challenging capital. When employers demand workers' concessions by threatening to close or relocate enterprises abroad, unions could refuse and instead establish worker co-ops.

Localities in the US could use the legal right of eminent domain to purchase private property for a "community purpose", such as organizing and supporting worker co-ops. Such community purposes could be—as they historically have been—to obtain land and other resources for worker co-ops as part of strategies to mitigate unemployment and poverty.

High school, college, and university curricula could include lessons and discussions about how the US might do better than capitalism and offer practical courses for establishing worker coops. Business schools and college economics departments could integrate alternatives to capitalism into their curricula.

A politically encouraged form of transition could see progressive political forces ally with co-ops in systems of mutual support. Co-op organizations could be crucial connectors between an organized political left and workers' daily struggles inside enterprises. The worker cooperatives and their community supporters could provide support, labor power, and financial help to left political initiatives and campaigns. In return, the left could mobilize demonstrations, local ongoing meetings, and electoral campaigns to secure legislative frameworks, capital, and markets needed for allied worker-co-op partners to thrive and grow. Such partnerships could establish a sustained and sustainable economic base for left politics everywhere.

For transitions, it would help for the worker co-op sectors of today's economies to grow. Then, others can view worker co-ops in action: by learning how others experience life and labor within worker co-ops, by buying products from worker co-ops, and by living in communities whose economies include a significant worker-co-op sector. For people to make informed, democratic choices about capitalist versus cooperative workplaces, a functioning worker-co-op sector needs to be part of their environment. When people have and understand options, they make better individual and also social decisions.

For transition to a democratic economy, we need cooperative struc-tures and models, in theory and in practice, as so many paths forward. The more of them we build, the more ways for people to think about and experience that transition. Political movements and parties must speak about and fight for the political changes needed to establish and grow cooperatives in all sectors.

Transition will follow from alliances of capitalism's victims and critics as they pursue two conjoint projects: (1) to increase the social presence of alternative economic systems (worker co-ops) within a declining capitalism, and (2) to organize victims and critics of capitalism alongside members of worker co-ops into a combined political force committed to dispelling capitalism's myths and their hold on people. This political movement would offer solutions to capitalism's problems that include basic system change and transition to a better society.

Moving on from Capitalism

It is a critical time in human history. The effects of capitalism's inequality, instability, and inadequate response to climate change are converging into disasters. This will continue if we keep being led by a small minority of people interested, above all, in maintaining the profit-driven status quo that benefits them. Capitalism's last three centuries showed us that the fundamental changes we need proved impossible within the boundaries of the system.

In US media, classrooms, and governance, public discourse largely ignores how the capitalist class structure of production contributes to the intertwined declines of the US empire and its economy. No policy aimed at class change is permitted by the small minority of people who sit at the top of our society (at the peaks of our corporate organizations, as well as Republican and Democratic ones). Without knowing about class-focused policies, the public cannot think about or debate them. For capitalists, that is the point: keep class change away by keeping its possibilities and advantages out of sight and mind. To offset that is what this book attempts.

We cannot expect the capitalist system's mounting problems to vanish by themselves, as if magically, or by the action of our "leaders." The latter is a big part of the problems we face—a very small minority that deludes itself and the population as a whole. This minority cannot face the roots of its multiplying failures in capitalism itself. It falls to us to deal with capitalism's divided, and divisive, class structure of production. Serious attempts at basic social change require that we understand capitalism critically and act accordingly.

Capitalism, surplus, and class are crucial issues. The campaign to democratize today's enterprises addresses all those issues at a key point of their connection. That campaign is a key class struggle of our time, the practical fruit of understanding capitalism critically.